Eyewitness
ENERGY

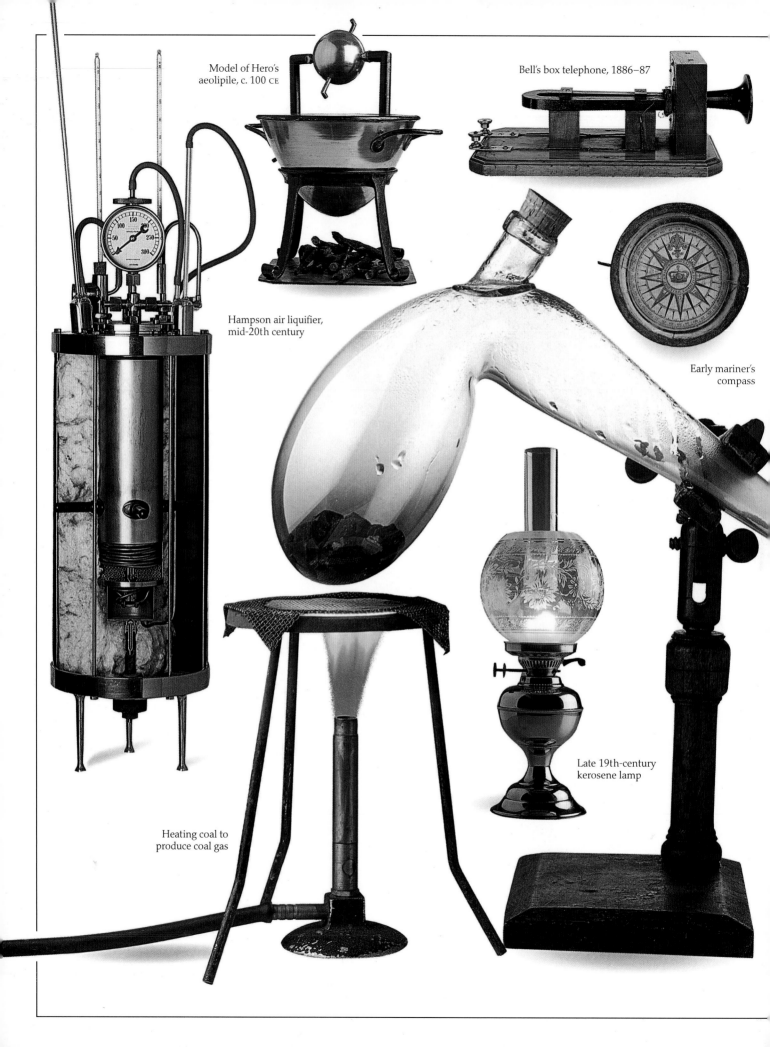

Model of Hero's
aeolipile, c. 100 CE

Bell's box telephone, 1886–87

Hampson air liquifier,
mid-20th century

Early mariner's
compass

Late 19th-century
kerosene lamp

Heating coal to
produce coal gas

Eyewitness
ENERGY

Written by
JACK CHALLONER

Late 19th-century
burning lens

Late 19th-century apparatus
to show that heat causes
expansion in solids

Model of a Greek ship of 800 BCE

Model of an early
20th-century tram

Model of a Pelton wheel,
late 19th century

Melting ice in
a hot liquid

DK Publishing

Late 19th-century electricity meter

Model of Huygens' pendulum timepiece of 1673

DK

LONDON, NEW YORK, MELBOURNE, MUNICH, and DELHI

Project editor Stephanie Jackson
Art editor Gurinder Purewall
Designer Marianna Papachrysanthou
Production Eunice Paterson
Managing editor Josephine Buchanan
Senior art editor Thomas Keenes
Picture researchers Deborah Pownall, Catherine O'Rourke
Special photography Clive Streeter
Editorial consultant Brian Bowers, Science Museum, London
US editor Charles A. Wills
US consultant Professor Warren Yasso
Teachers College, Columbia University

REVISED EDITION
Revised by Jack Challoner

DK INDIA
Project editor Nidhi Sharma
Project art editor Rajnish Kashyap
Editor Pallavi Singh
Designer Honlung Zach Ragui
Managing editor Saloni Talwar
Managing art editor Romi Chakraborty
DTP designer Tarun Sharma
Picture researcher Sumedha Chopra

DK UK
Senior editor Rob Houston
Senior art editor Philip Letsu
Production editor Adam Stoneham
Production controller Rebecca Short
Publisher Andrew Macintyre

DK US
US editor Margaret Parrish
Editorial director Nancy Ellwood

This edition published in the United States in 2012
by DK Publishing, 375 Hudson Street, New York, New York 10014
First published in the United States in 1993

10 9 8 7 6 5 4 3 2 1
001—183528—July/12

DK books are available at special discounts when purchased in
bulk for sales promotions, premiums, fundraising, or educational use.
For details, contact: DK Publishing Special Markets
375 Hudson Street, New York, New York 10014
SpecialSales@dk.com

A catalog record for this book is available
from the Library of Congress.

ISBN: 978-0-7566-9300-8 (Hardcover)
ISBN: 978-0-7566-9301-5 (Library binding)-

Color reproduction by Colorscan, Singapore
Printed and bound in China by Toppan Printing Co. (Shenzhen) Ltd.

Discover more at
www.dk.com

Late 19th-century thermometer

Boys' gas calorimeter, early 20th century

Contents

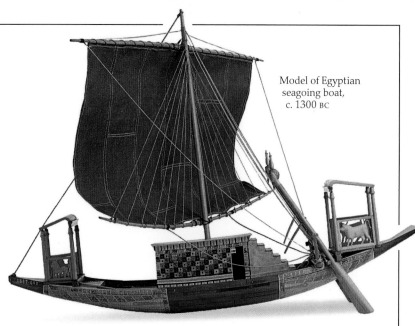

Model of Egyptian
seagoing boat,
c. 1300 BC

What is energy?

WITHOUT ENERGY, there would be nothing. There would be no Sun, no wind, no rivers, and no life at all. Energy is everywhere, and energy changing from one form to another is behind everything that happens. Energy, defined as the ability to make things happen, cannot be created. Nor can it be destroyed. Plants and animals harness energy from nature to help them grow and survive. The most intelligent of animals, human beings, have developed many ways of using the available energy to improve their lifestyle. Ancient people used energy from fire (pp. 10–11), and they developed tools to use energy from their muscles (pp. 8–9) more effectively. But ancient people did not understand the role of energy in their lives. Such an understanding of energy has really developed only over the past few hundred years.

THE FAITHFUL SUN
The Sun (pp. 48–49) supplies nearly all the energy on Earth. The energy from the Sun travels through 93 million miles (150 million km) of space to Earth as electromagnetic radiation (pp. 40–41), a form of energy that includes light, X-rays, and radio waves.

AN ENERGETIC FROG
This frog needs energy to jump. Because anything that moves has energy (pp. 16–17), energy is needed to start the frog moving. The frog gets the energy it needs from food (pp. 52–53). When the frog lands, it will lose the energy of its movement. But the energy will still exist as heat (pp. 20–21) in its body and in the surrounding soil, air, and water.

A BRIGHT SPARK
On a hot and humid day, electrical energy builds up as electric charges separate in the clouds. When the separation is large enough, there is enough energy to spark from the cloud down to the ground in an impressive display. The electrical energy becomes the heat energy and light energy of lightning, and the sound energy of thunder.

ENERGY UNDERGROUND
The energy released by this geyser did not come from the Sun. It came from the heat of molten rock in the Earth and heat generated by friction and pressure as the rocks deep underground push against each other. In some places, people use the heat energy generated in this way as an alternative to fossil fuels (pp. 54–55) for heating homes or generating electricity (pp. 58–59).

SEETHING VOLCANO
Huge amounts of energy are released in a large volcanic eruption. This painting of the eruption of Mount Vesuvius in Italy shows molten lava, smoke, poisonous gas, and ashes being blown into the air. In 79 CE, the volcano erupted, covering the towns of Herculaneum and Pompeii with debris.

CARNIVOROUS PLANT
Animals need to obtain
their energy by eating other
living things. But most plants
can store energy directly from the Sun
by a process called photosynthesis (pp. 50–51).
When sunlight falls on a plant, it causes chemical
reactions, which result in energy being stored in
chemicals within the plant. Some plants, such as this
Venus fly-trap, supplement their energy by attracting
insects—they digest the insects, making use of the
energy and chemicals stored in the insect's body.

ENERGY FROM THE WIND
Energy is needed to make these trees bend. As the Sun
heats the Earth, it does so unevenly because some parts of
the Earth heat up more quickly than others. This causes
differences in air pressure, and high-pressure air moves to
equalize with lower-pressure air, creating winds. So the energy
from wind (pp. 12–13) is actually energy from the Sun.

ENERGY IN RUNNING WATER
As the Sun's energy warms the seas and
rivers, some of the water evaporates, and it
rises high into the atmosphere where
it condenses to form clouds. The water
droplets in the clouds gather and fall
back to Earth as raindrops. The rain
gathers into fast-moving streams
(pp. 12–13). Therefore, the
energy of running water comes
originally from the Sun.

Muscle energy

IN ANCIENT TIMES, PEOPLE USED THE ENERGY of their own muscles to do work such as gathering food and building shelter. To make this muscle energy even more useful, and use it efficiently, early people invented simple tools. The first tools were made of wood and stone, but once smelting was developed (pp. 10–11) metal tools became available. Another source of muscle power was found in animals—one large animal, such as an ox, can be up to seven times more powerful than one human. Animals were used on their own for transporting people and goods, but they were also used together with simple tools and machines to perform more complex tasks, such as plowing the ground and pumping water for irrigation. By making more use of this kind of muscle energy, people had more time to develop other skills and activities.

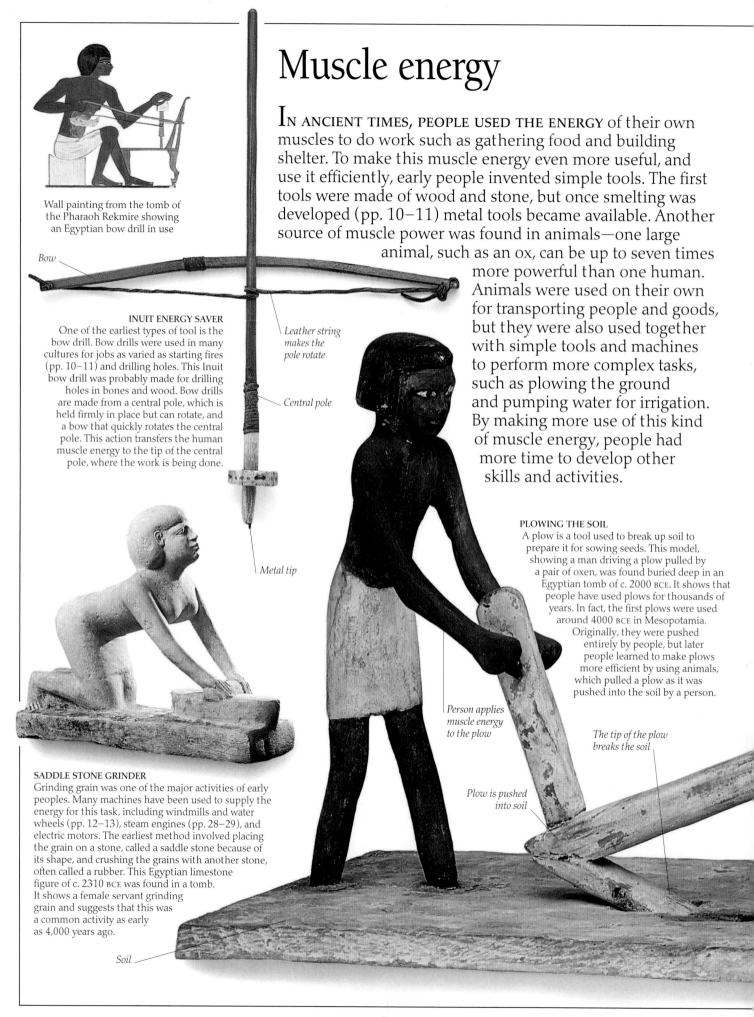

Wall painting from the tomb of the Pharaoh Rekmire showing an Egyptian bow drill in use

Bow

INUIT ENERGY SAVER
One of the earliest types of tool is the bow drill. Bow drills were used in many cultures for jobs as varied as starting fires (pp. 10–11) and drilling holes. This Inuit bow drill was probably made for drilling holes in bones and wood. Bow drills are made from a central pole, which is held firmly in place but can rotate, and a bow that quickly rotates the central pole. This action transfers the human muscle energy to the tip of the central pole, where the work is being done.

Leather string makes the pole rotate

Central pole

Metal tip

SADDLE STONE GRINDER
Grinding grain was one of the major activities of early peoples. Many machines have been used to supply the energy for this task, including windmills and water wheels (pp. 12–13), steam engines (pp. 28–29), and electric motors. The earliest method involved placing the grain on a stone, called a saddle stone because of its shape, and crushing the grains with another stone, often called a rubber. This Egyptian limestone figure of c. 2310 BCE was found in a tomb. It shows a female servant grinding grain and suggests that this was a common activity as early as 4,000 years ago.

PLOWING THE SOIL
A plow is a tool used to break up soil to prepare it for sowing seeds. This model, showing a man driving a plow pulled by a pair of oxen, was found buried deep in an Egyptian tomb of c. 2000 BCE. It shows that people have used plows for thousands of years. In fact, the first plows were used around 4000 BCE in Mesopotamia. Originally, they were pushed entirely by people, but later people learned to make plows more efficient by using animals, which pulled a plow as it was pushed into the soil by a person.

Person applies muscle energy to the plow

The tip of the plow breaks the soil

Plow is pushed into soil

Soil

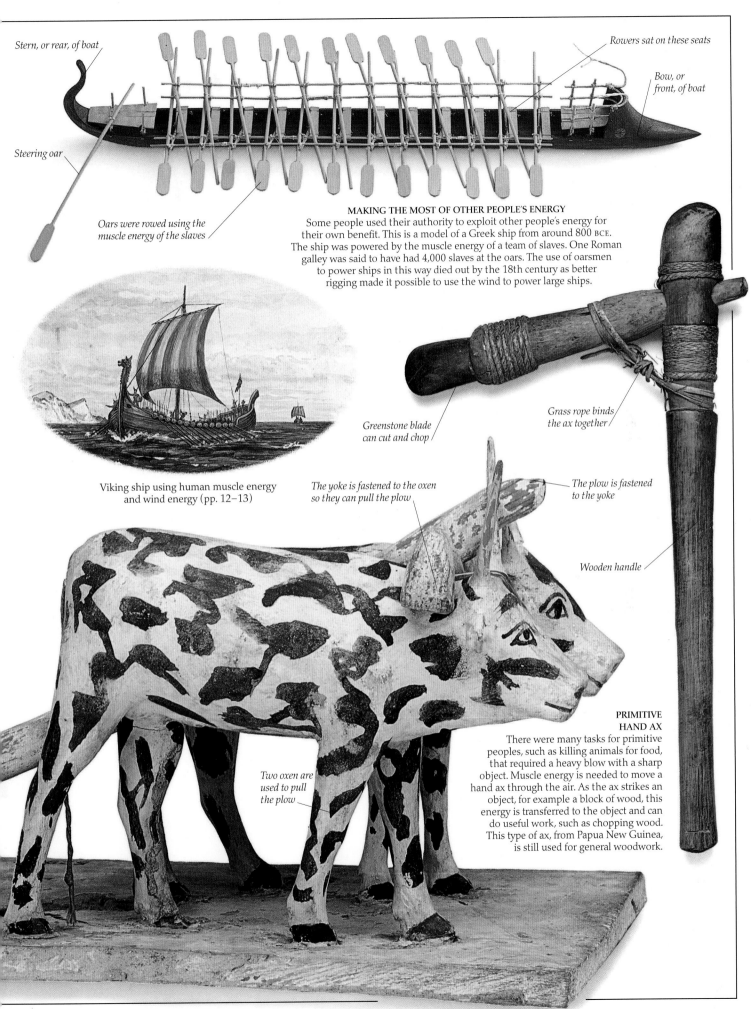

Stern, or rear, of boat

Steering oar

Rowers sat on these seats

Bow, or front, of boat

Oars were rowed using the muscle energy of the slaves

MAKING THE MOST OF OTHER PEOPLE'S ENERGY

Some people used their authority to exploit other people's energy for their own benefit. This is a model of a Greek ship from around 800 BCE. The ship was powered by the muscle energy of a team of slaves. One Roman galley was said to have had 4,000 slaves at the oars. The use of oarsmen to power ships in this way died out by the 18th century as better rigging made it possible to use the wind to power large ships.

Viking ship using human muscle energy and wind energy (pp. 12–13)

Greenstone blade can cut and chop

Grass rope binds the ax together

The yoke is fastened to the oxen so they can pull the plow

The plow is fastened to the yoke

Wooden handle

Two oxen are used to pull the plow

PRIMITIVE HAND AX

There were many tasks for primitive peoples, such as killing animals for food, that required a heavy blow with a sharp object. Muscle energy is needed to move a hand ax through the air. As the ax strikes an object, for example a block of wood, this energy is transferred to the object and can do useful work, such as chopping wood. This type of ax, from Papua New Guinea, is still used for general woodwork.

Energy from fire

MYTHS ABOUT FIRE
The energy released by burning fuels was an extremely important resource for early people. But even though fire was used every day, they did not understand what it really was. To them, fire was magic. Throughout the world, different cultures had different ideas to explain where fire came from. Some said it was given by the gods. This statue is of Xuihtecuhtli, the Aztec Lord of Fire. His image was placed in the hearth of every home.

HUMAN BEINGS HAVE USED FIRE for thousands of years, though the date of the discovery or first use of fire is unknown. It is known, however, that late Stone Age cave-dwellers kept their caves warm with fires, which, it seems, were kept alight continuously for months or years. Since then, people have learned to use the energy of fire in many ways, from cooking food and lighting their homes, to smelting ore, firing pottery, and making glass. Most of the energy from fire is heat energy (pp. 20–21) that is released when a fuel is burned. The first fuel was wood, but charcoal, which is produced by heating wood without air, burns with a hotter flame. Burning charcoal and using bellows to increase the supply of air causes the charcoal to burn hotter, making it possible to extract metals from their ores. The metal atoms in metal ores are usually bound tightly to oxygen atoms, and energy from fire is needed to separate them into oxygen plus the pure metal. Although most of the energy of fire is heat, energy in the form of light and sound is also released. This is why fire can be seen, felt, and heard.

FIRE FOR COOKING
From evidence found in caves in Europe and Asia, archeologists have concluded that our ancestors began using fire for cooking at least 250,000 years ago. The heat energy from fire can be used to change food in many ways. It can make meat more tender, and it can make food safer to eat by killing harmful bacteria. Also, the heat of a fire can help combine ingredients into new substances, as it does when dough is baked into bread.

SMELTING THE ORE
Ores are rocks that contain metals, but not in a pure state. Energy is needed to extract, or "smelt," metals from their ores. The metal atoms are tightly combined with atoms of other elements, such as oxygen. The energy that fire supplies breaks the metal from its bonds with the other elements. The first metals to be smelted were copper and tin, which people later learned to combine to make bronze. All metals need a high temperature to be smelted, and the use of bellows helps to reach this by increasing the supply of air to the fire. This is a model of a primitive hearth from Sudan in Africa. A hearth like this one can reach temperatures of around 1,650° F (900° C). In some parts of central Africa, smelting hearths are still used.

Sticks operate the bellows

Bellows increase the supply of air to the fire

Charcoal is the fuel for the fire

Metal ore is placed in the fire

Smelted metal is left at the bottom of the fire

Upper level is cooler

Containers for cooling glass slowly

Ceramic pots hold the batch for melting

Blowpipe is inserted through one of these windows

Wood fire is burned at the bottom of the furnace

GLASSMAKER'S FURNACE

Fire is an essential element in making glass. The main ingredient of glass is sand, which is mixed with other ingredients to form the "batch." The batch is melted by the heat from fire, and when it is cooled, the glass is formed. A fire raged at the bottom of this 16th-century furnace, and the batch was melted in large ceramic pots. A glass blower could then reach through one of the windows and pick up some of the molten mixture at the end of a "blowpipe," which was then used to blow the glass into the desired shape. A mold could also be used to help achieve this. Glass was first made as long ago as 4000 BCE, and there is evidence to show that it was blown in this way during the 1st century BCE.

ROMAN UNDERFLOOR HEATING

Fire has been used to heat homes for many thousands of years. The ancient Greeks were the first to use underfloor heating, but the Romans improved on it with a sophisticated heating system called a "hypocaust." It heated the rooms of public bathhouses and some houses. A fire was lit and tended by a slave, and the hot air from the fire moved around in ducts under the floors, eventually escaping through a chimney. This potentially dangerous use of fire in the home may have been one of the reasons the Romans were also the first to have organized firefighters.

Roman glass bottles, c. 3–4th century CE

Bellows are made of leather and clay

Energy from wind and water

ANCIENT PEOPLE COULD SEE that there was tremendous force in the natural motion of wind and water. Although they had no scientific understanding of energy, they realized that they could harness these natural forces to do some heavy work. Early civilizations used "mechanical energy" to do work like lifting, grinding grain, building, and transporting people and goods (pp. 8–9). This mechanical energy could be obtained from wind or moving water. Wind and water flow are the most visible examples of natural energy on Earth, but that energy originally comes from the Sun (pp. 48–49). The wind that turns the sails of a windmill and fills the sails of a sailing boat is caused by the Sun heating the Earth. The rain that falls from the sky was once ocean, lake, or river water that evaporated into the atmosphere because of the Sun's energy.

ENERGY FOR THE DAILY GRIND
Horizontal water wheels like this are called "Greek" or "Norse" wheels. This wheel was used to grind grain into flour. Grain was placed into the top of the funnel-shaped container, called a hopper, and fell down between the millstones. The top millstone was turned by the water wheel underneath, and the grain was crushed to make flour, which fell down into the trough below. Horizontal wheels like this need fast-moving water to be effective.

Water power

Water wheels were used for irrigation as long ago as 600 BCE, but water power was first used for grinding corn around 100 BCE in various parts of the world. The type of water wheel used depended on how fast the stream or river flowed. The use of water power has since developed in many different ways and it is still an important alternative to fossil fuels (pp. 58–59).

Gears transfer mechanical energy to different parts of the mill

Belts are attached to pulleys

Reels hold the cotton

USING WATER IN INDUSTRY
Until the invention of the steam engine (pp. 28–29), water power was heavily used in industry. This model shows a cotton mill that was built at the end of the 18th century. Water flowed underneath the mill, turning the water wheel. The movement of the water was a reliable and free source of energy, and it powered the machines in the mill through gears and pulleys. To make use of water, such mills had to be built near rivers. Steam engines, in contrast, could be used anywhere— one of the main reasons steam power took over in industry.

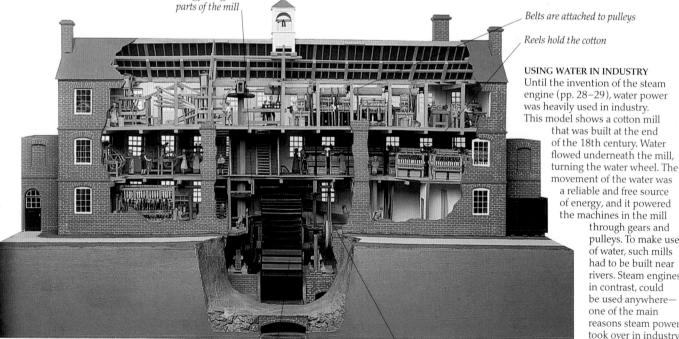

Undershot water wheel

Belts transmit the power from the water wheel to the machines

The wheel moves in the direction of the water flow

Water falls into the water wheel

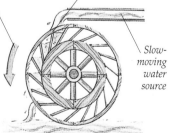

OVERSHOT WHEEL
Overshot water wheels are used where water falls from a great height, having potential energy (pp. 14–15), but is slow moving, having little kinetic energy (pp. 16–17). The water pulls one side of the wheel around with it as the water falls.

Slow-moving water source

UNDERSHOT WHEEL
These water wheels are used in fast-moving water, which has a lot of kinetic energy (pp. 16–17). The water passes under the wheel and pushes blades, which turn the wheel. This could be connected to heavy machinery in factories.

The wheel moves in the direction of the water flow

Fast-moving water source

Wind power

One of the earliest forms of power that people learned to use, wind was used to move boats with cloth sails as long ago as 3500 BCE. On land, the first windmills seem to have been used in Persia around 700 CE. The sails turned horizontally and were connected directly to grindstones used to grind grain. Wind power is also used for irrigating dry land and draining wet land, and as an alternative energy source to generate electricity.

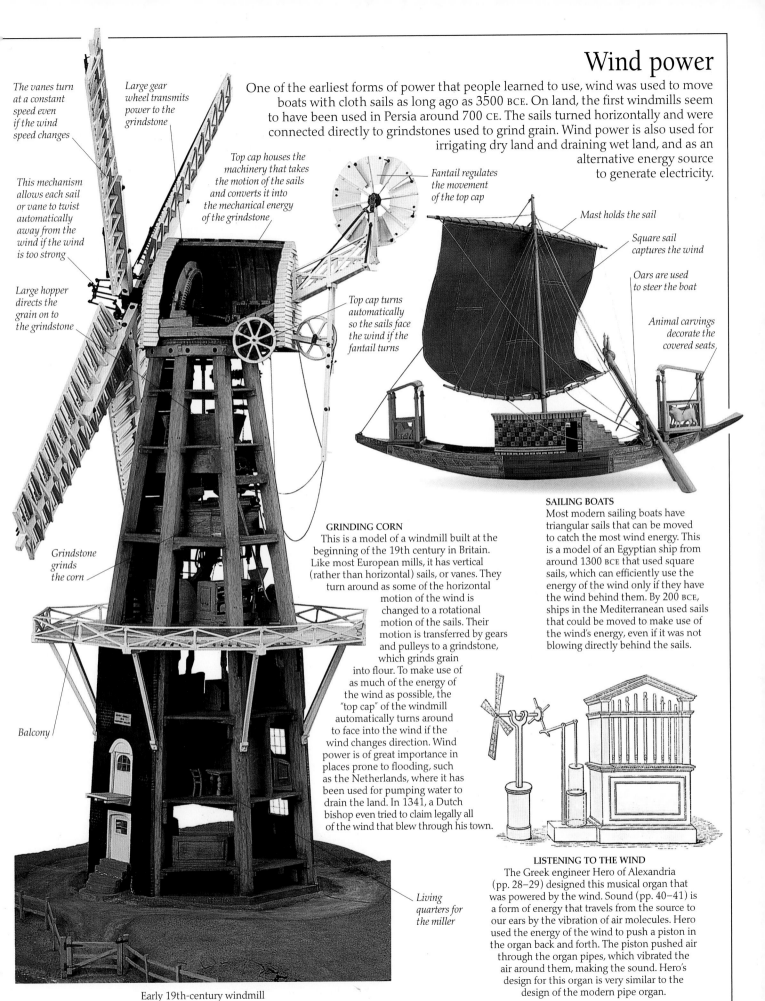

The vanes turn at a constant speed even if the wind speed changes

Large gear wheel transmits power to the grindstone

This mechanism allows each sail or vane to twist automatically away from the wind if the wind is too strong

Top cap houses the machinery that takes the motion of the sails and converts it into the mechanical energy of the grindstone

Fantail regulates the movement of the top cap

Mast holds the sail

Square sail captures the wind

Large hopper directs the grain on to the grindstone

Top cap turns automatically so the sails face the wind if the fantail turns

Oars are used to steer the boat

Animal carvings decorate the covered seats

Grindstone grinds the corn

Balcony

Living quarters for the miller

Early 19th-century windmill

GRINDING CORN
This is a model of a windmill built at the beginning of the 19th century in Britain. Like most European mills, it has vertical (rather than horizontal) sails, or vanes. They turn around as some of the horizontal motion of the wind is changed to a rotational motion of the sails. Their motion is transferred by gears and pulleys to a grindstone, which grinds grain into flour. To make use of as much of the energy of the wind as possible, the "top cap" of the windmill automatically turns around to face into the wind if the wind changes direction. Wind power is of great importance in places prone to flooding, such as the Netherlands, where it has been used for pumping water to drain the land. In 1341, a Dutch bishop even tried to claim legally all of the wind that blew through his town.

SAILING BOATS
Most modern sailing boats have triangular sails that can be moved to catch the most wind energy. This is a model of an Egyptian ship from around 1300 BCE that used square sails, which can efficiently use the energy of the wind only if they have the wind behind them. By 200 BCE, ships in the Mediterranean used sails that could be moved to make use of the wind's energy, even if it was not blowing directly behind the sails.

LISTENING TO THE WIND
The Greek engineer Hero of Alexandria (pp. 28–29) designed this musical organ that was powered by the wind. Sound (pp. 40–41) is a form of energy that travels from the source to our ears by the vibration of air molecules. Hero used the energy of the wind to push a piston in the organ back and forth. The piston pushed air through the organ pipes, which vibrated the air around them, making the sound. Hero's design for this organ is very similar to the design of the modern pipe organ.

Potential energy

<small>*Hands turn slowly with the release of energy from the falling weight*</small>

A<small>N EGG THAT IS RELEASED</small> from some height on to a hard surface will fall, and it will probably break. Before the egg is released, it has the "potential" to fall. People know that an egg released from a height will fall, and most people also realize that the higher and the heavier the egg, the greater the chance that it will break. But where does the egg's potential to fall come from? Someone may have lifted it up, working against gravity and using the energy in their muscles from the food they have eaten (pp. 52–53) to do so. Potential energy is stored whenever something moves in the opposite direction to a force acting on it. So, stretching a rubber band stores energy because the molecules of the rubber band are moved apart, working against the forces between the molecules that are pulling them together. There are many forms of potential energy, and many forms of energy that it can become. But the total amount of energy remains the same (pp. 24–25).

HUYGENS' CLOCK
Dutch scientist Christian Huygens (1629–95) was the inventor of the pendulum clock, which he first devised by attaching a pendulum to the gears of a mechanical clock. The regular swing of the pendulum made the clock run much more precisely than before. This is a model of a clock Huygens made in 1673. The energy to drive the hands of this clock against friction comes from the falling of the lead weight, which releases a fraction of the weight's potential energy with each tick. The clock stops when the weight reaches its lowest position. The energy, or "work," of the person who raises the weight is stored in the weight as potential energy, which is released as the weight descends.

POTENTIAL ENERGY AT WAR
These Roman soldiers are storing their muscle energy in a catapult. When the catapult is released, the potential energy that the soldiers contributed is released. The catapult will shoot a missile forward toward the enemy, using all of its stored potential energy.

<small>*Small weight acts as a counter-balance, keeping the string tight*</small>

<small>*Lead weight loses potential energy as it descends*</small>

WINDING UP THE CLOCK
Inside a mechanical clock is a coiled piece of metal called a "mainspring." The mainspring stores the muscle energy of the person who winds the clock. The clock can run for a few days by releasing the potential energy stored in the mainspring. This clock mechanism transforms this energy into the movement of the hands, the sound of the ticking, and a small amount of heat (pp. 20–21). Many other types of clock, such as water clocks or candle clocks, rely on the steady release of some form of potential energy to keep time. Many scientists used to think the universe was like a huge clockwork machine, gradually winding down as time passes.

<small>*Key is used to transfer energy from the muscles to the clock*</small>

<small>*Gearing inside the clock mechanism controls the release of the energy*</small>

<small>*Pendulum is kept swinging by the energy of the falling weight*</small>

GRANDFATHER CLOCK
A grandfather clock is a large clock that is housed in a freestanding case. This one has three dials, all driven by the energy of the falling weights.

STUDYING IMPACT

Although it was not until the mid-19th century that people really understood potential energy, it was the subject of many experiments carried out during the century before. In this experiment Dutch scientist Willem 's Gravesand (pp. 16–17) studied potential energy by dropping balls of various weights on to soft clay. He found that the impact the balls made in the clay depended on the weight of the balls and the height from which the balls fell. In other words, the potential of the balls to make an impact was greater for heavier balls and for those dropped from a greater height. 's Gravesand also experimented with the energy stored in springs, and he built machines to measure and demonstrate the properties of moving objects.

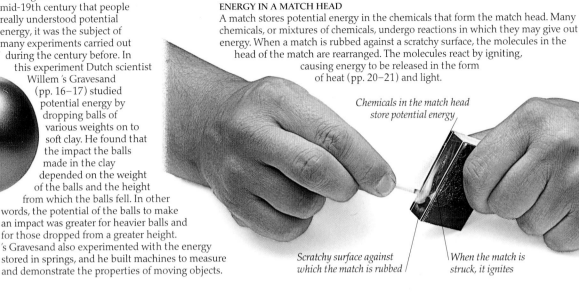

Metal ball

ENERGY IN A MATCH HEAD

A match stores potential energy in the chemicals that form the match head. Many chemicals, or mixtures of chemicals, undergo reactions in which they may give out energy. When a match is rubbed against a scratchy surface, the molecules in the head of the match are rearranged. The molecules react by igniting, causing energy to be released in the form of heat (pp. 20–21) and light.

Chemicals in the match head store potential energy

Scratchy surface against which the match is rubbed

When the match is struck, it ignites

Soft clay to record the impact of the ball

The size of the dent can now be measured

The ball has lost its potential energy

1 POTENTIAL ENERGY

The metal ball is suspended over some soft clay. The ball has been weighed beforehand, and now its height over the clay is measured. In order to release the potential energy stored in the ball, the string must be cut.

2 THE ENERGY OF IMPACT

The impact in the clay shows the amount of kinetic energy (pp. 16–17) of the ball as it hit the clay. The kinetic energy of an object increases as it accelerates. If the ball had twice the weight, it would have made twice the impact.

GALILEO GALILEI

One of the first modern physicists was Galileo Galilei (1564–1642), an Italian scholar. He experimented with objects falling and rolling down slopes. Although he could not have understood the idea of energy, he seemed to have a natural grasp of the idea of potential energy. This was truly remarkable because, at the time, everyone else followed the ideas of Aristotle (pp. 16–17), who thought that objects moved because it was "in their nature to do so." By combining careful experimentation and brilliant reasoning, Galileo showed that this view was incorrect. Objects fall not just because they are heavy, but because they are given potential energy—perhaps by someone lifting them. Without Galileo, it may have taken much longer to realize this.

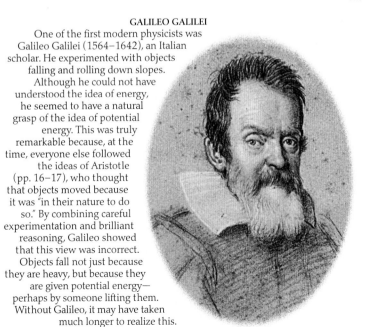

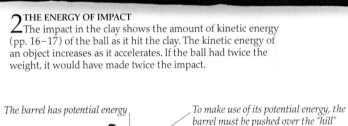

The barrel has potential energy

To make use of its potential energy, the barrel must be pushed over the "hill"

The barrel has used its supply of potential energy

POTENTIAL HILL

Energy is needed to move any object against the force of gravity, which tries to pull the object down. To get a barrel to the top of a hill, muscle energy must be applied to move the barrel. When the barrel rolls down the hill, it gradually loses its potential energy until it reaches its lowest potential energy at the bottom of the slope. Natural processes act in the same way, always finding their lowest energy. Notice the shape of the hill—it has a bump over which the barrel must be pushed before its potential energy can be released. Many chemical reactions, such as the burning of matches (see top), also have a potential energy "hill"—they must be given energy to start, but then they continue of their own accord. For matches, the energy to get over the hill is supplied by the heat produced when the matches are struck.

The energy of movement

EVERYTHING THAT MOVES HAS ENERGY called "kinetic" energy. The faster an object moves and the more mass it has, the more kinetic energy it has. In 1686, the German mathematician Gottfried Wilhelm Leibniz (1646–1716) introduced the term *vis viva*, meaning living force, which was very close to the idea of kinetic energy that was figured out in the 1800s. The *vis viva* of an object depended on its mass and speed. Scientists noticed that this energy seemed to be "conserved"—a moving ball could transfer its energy to a stationary one. However, when a moving object hits a soft material, such as sand, it is obvious that the energy is not conserved because the sand seems to absorb the movement. This puzzle remained unsolved until it was shown that moving objects have energy that can be changed into other forms (pp. 24–25). Thus, when a moving object hits sand the energy is not lost, but changed into a form such as heat. All forms of energy are either kinetic or potential energy (pp.14–15).

WHAT THE GREEKS THOUGHT

The Greek philosopher Aristotle (384–322 BCE) thought that things move toward their "natural place" because of their nature. A stone is heavy, so it will fall. It is in a bird's nature to fly. Because these ideas seemed correct, no one tested them to find out whether they were true. Indeed, it was nearly 2,000 years later that people started experimenting with objects in motion and challenging Aristotle's view.

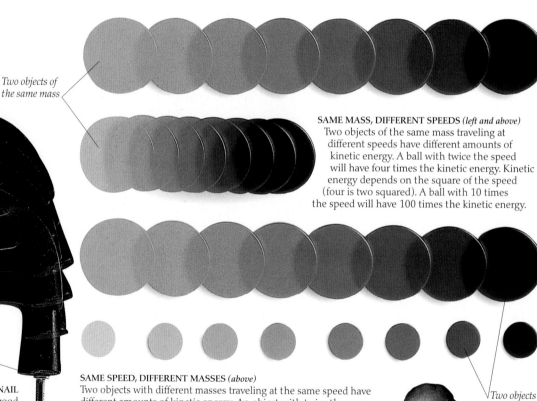

Two objects of the same mass

SAME MASS, DIFFERENT SPEEDS (*left and above*)

Two objects of the same mass traveling at different speeds have different amounts of kinetic energy. A ball with twice the speed will have four times the kinetic energy. Kinetic energy depends on the square of the speed (four is two squared). A ball with 10 times the speed will have 100 times the kinetic energy.

Moving hammer has a lot of kinetic energy

The kinetic energy of the hammer is transferred to the nail

HAMMERING THE NAIL

The head of a hammer has a good deal of kinetic energy as it strikes a nail. Once the hammer comes to a stop it has lost all of its kinetic energy. But the energy has not disappeared. It has been transferred to the atoms and molecules of the nail, the wood, the air, and even the hammer. This random kinetic energy is heat (pp.20–21).

The energy the nail gains is transferred to the wood

SAME SPEED, DIFFERENT MASSES (*above*)

Two objects with different masses traveling at the same speed have different amounts of kinetic energy. An object with twice the mass will have twice the kinetic energy. The mass of an object is the amount of matter it is made of, and mass is directly related to weight, which is the force of gravity pulling on an object.

Two objects of different masses

SCIENTISTS IN CONFLICT

Through the 18th century there was a great deal of argument about Leibniz's idea of *vis viva*. One person involved in this controversy was Gabrielle de Breteuil, Marquise du Châtelet (c. 1700–49). Many scientists rejected the idea of *vis viva*, but the Marquise was convinced that Leibniz was right. In 1740, she wrote a book that convinced many others that the *vis viva* idea was correct.

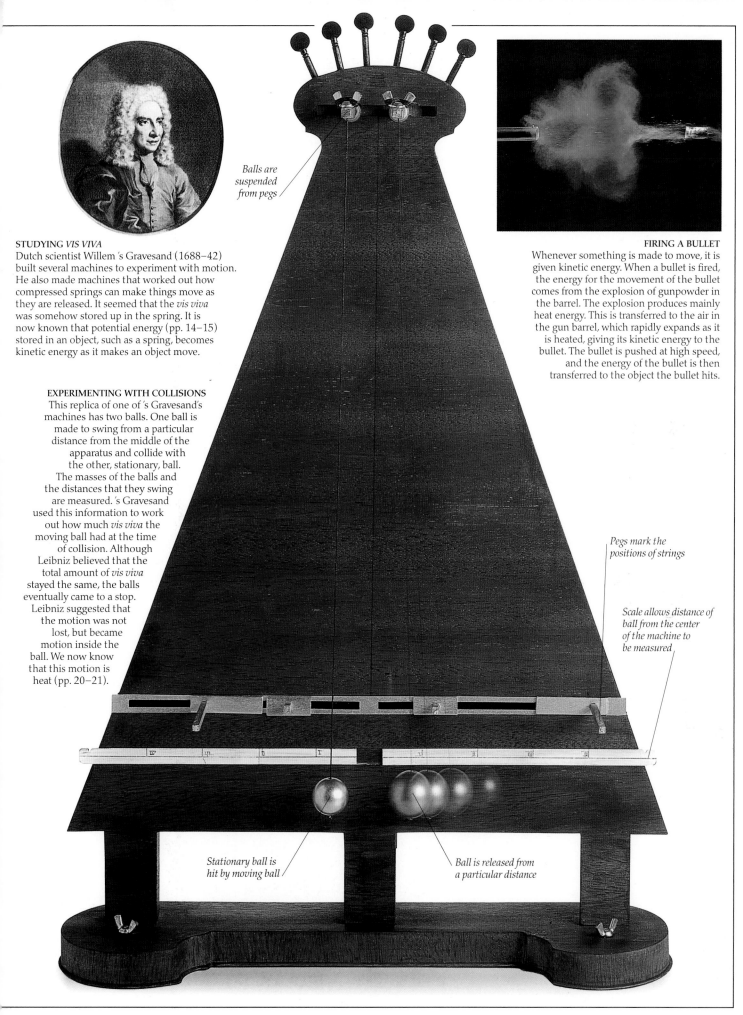

STUDYING *VIS VIVA*
Dutch scientist Willem 's Gravesand (1688–42) built several machines to experiment with motion. He also made machines that worked out how compressed springs can make things move as they are released. It seemed that the *vis viva* was somehow stored up in the spring. It is now known that potential energy (pp. 14–15) stored in an object, such as a spring, becomes kinetic energy as it makes an object move.

Balls are suspended from pegs

EXPERIMENTING WITH COLLISIONS
This replica of one of 's Gravesand's machines has two balls. One ball is made to swing from a particular distance from the middle of the apparatus and collide with the other, stationary, ball. The masses of the balls and the distances that they swing are measured. 's Gravesand used this information to work out how much *vis viva* the moving ball had at the time of collision. Although Leibniz believed that the total amount of *vis viva* stayed the same, the balls eventually came to a stop. Leibniz suggested that the motion was not lost, but became motion inside the ball. We now know that this motion is heat (pp. 20–21).

FIRING A BULLET
Whenever something is made to move, it is given kinetic energy. When a bullet is fired, the energy for the movement of the bullet comes from the explosion of gunpowder in the barrel. The explosion produces mainly heat energy. This is transferred to the air in the gun barrel, which rapidly expands as it is heated, giving its kinetic energy to the bullet. The bullet is pushed at high speed, and the energy of the bullet is then transferred to the object the bullet hits.

Pegs mark the positions of strings

Scale allows distance of ball from the center of the machine to be measured

Stationary ball is hit by moving ball

Ball is released from a particular distance

Imponderable fluids

MOST SCIENTISTS of the 18th century believed that matter was made of particles. Many of them thought that effects such as light, heat, magnetism, and electricity were also made of particles. These "effects" were known to travel from place to place. Scientists thought that to do this, the particles had to flow like fluid, be weightless (experiments to weigh heat and electricity were unsuccessful), and be able to penetrate objects. Each phenomenon was thought to be carried by different fluids, which were called "imponderable fluids," so they would be completely separate. The greatest interest was in heat (pp. 20–21) and electricity (pp. 22–23), and further study of these effects led in part to the downfall of this theory. By the middle of the 19th century the idea of imponderable fluids was proven to be incorrect (pp. 20–21).

Hand is placed on top of glass globe to produce a glow

ELECTRICAL FLUID

At the beginning of the 18th century, Francis Hauksbee (c. 1666–1713) was in London, England, investigating the effects of electricity. He made a machine with a glass globe from which most of the air was removed. When the globe was rotated and a hand was placed on top of the globe, electricity was produced, often giving a strange glow. Hauksbee thought the glow was caused by electrical fluid. Using this machine, he also observed that threads hung around or inside the globe were stiffened by the electricity, as if a fluid were escaping from them.

Hauksbee's drawing shows that the threads become stiff as electrical fluid escapes

A large wheel rotates the globe very quickly even when the handle is turned very slowly

Turning the handle rotates the glass globe

SCIENTIFIC INVESTIGATOR

Isaac Newton (1642–1727) investigated the behavior of the natural world, but he did not try to explain why things behave as they do. However, he did seem to favor the idea that light was made up of particles of "fire." Although he died before the imponderable fluid theory became popular, Newton continued to have a huge influence on scientists, and many of his ideas were said to be in favor of imponderable fluids.

Hauksbee's "Barometric Light Experiment"

The ring is moveable and passes easily over the ball

Particle of matter

Particle of fluid

Fluid passing between objects

Matter with high fluid concentration   Matter with low fluid concentration

RING AND BALL

During the 18th century, scientific demonstrations became very popular. One reason so many people supported the imponderable fluid theory was that it seemed to explain their observations. In one famous demonstration, a cold metal ball that just fit through a ring would not fit through the same ring after the ball was heated. This was explained by the idea that heat was a fluid made of particles, which entered the ball and made it bigger.

The ring is moved away so that it will not get hot

The flame of the Bunsen burner heats the ball

FLUID MADE OF PARTICLES OF FIRE

Many people thought the fluids carrying light, electricity, and heat were made of particles of fire. Heat fluid is hot, light is given off by hot objects, and electricity makes hot sparks. The particles of these fluids penetrated between the particles of matter, and they pushed each other and the matter particles apart. Fluid could pass between objects containing more or less concentrated fluid.

This could explain why hot objects lost their heat to colder ones, for example.

The metal has been tarnished by the flame

The ball has expanded, and the ring no longer passes over it

1 SMALL BALL

In the first stage of this experiment, the ball is cold, and the ring passes over it easily. The ball is a solid, and it is composed of trillions of closely packed particles.

2 ADDING FLUID

The ball is heated by a hot flame. Particles of heat fluid were thought to pass from the flame into the ball. The hotter the ball becomes, the more heat fluid it contains.

3 FILLED WITH FLUID

The ball has expanded so much that the ring cannot pass over it. It was thought that particles of the metal were pushed apart as particles of heat fluid were crammed between them.

ELECTRICAL FLUID

American scientist Benjamin Franklin (1706–90) is famous for demonstrating that lightning is electrical. He flew a kite in a thunderstorm and observed what happened when a lightning bolt struck the kite. The lightning was conducted to the ground, behaving just like sparks made in his laboratory. Franklin showed that lightning is caused by electricity, but he mistakenly thought it was carried by a fluid.

ELECTRIFIED SOCKS

There were many observations made about the effects of electricity. People could make it, store it, and pass sparks of it between objects. In 1758, Robert Symmer (c. 1707–63) noticed that his silk socks behaved in a strange way when he took them off. They produced sparks and would often fill out, like a wind sock in a strong wind. The socks seemed to be filled with electrical fluid that produced sparks as it passed from his leg to the socks. These effects are actually caused by static electricity (pp. 22–23), an imbalance of electrical charge between the body and the socks.

Heat energy

FORGING WITH FIRE
Fire (pp. 10–11) has been used by humans for thousands of years to provide light, warmth, and the heat needed for cooking and smelting. Forging is the art of heating metal in fire and then hammering it into shapes, such as horseshoes.

DURING THE 18TH CENTURY, most scientists thought that heat was a fluid—and that temperature was the concentration of the fluid contained inside an object. But those ideas could not explain how friction produces heat. When you rub things together, some energy is passed on to the atoms and molecules of the things being rubbed. This is why friction "heats up" things (temperature is related to the motion of the particles of matter), atoms, and molecules. The more kinetic energy per particle, the hotter something is. The fluid theory of heat also could not explain why the temperature of melting ice stays the same, even though it is taking in heat. In this case, the heat energy causes the water molecules to break apart, so they can move independently as a liquid. All kinds of energy, including sound, light, and chemical energy, can end up as heat. The study of heat was crucial in formulating the scientific theory of energy (pp. 24–25).

This side shows Celsius

This side shows Fahrenheit

The alcohol inside the tube expands as its molecules move more quickly

The calcium oxide and water are mixed together in this vessel

Cold water

HEAT FROM CHEMICALS
When chemical reactions take place there is often a rise or fall in temperature, as heat energy is released or taken in. Some reactions need an energy input in order to take place. Others give out energy, as when water is added to calcium oxide, or quicklime. As the molecules of the two substances rearrange to form a new substance, calcium hydroxide, they release chemical potential energy (pp. 14–15), which had been stored between them. The released energy makes the atoms and molecules move more quickly, so the temperature rises.

Steam condenses on the inside of the flask

MEASURING TEMPERATURE
The temperature of any substance is directly related to the average kinetic energy (pp. 16–17) of the atoms or molecules of which it is made. Although the lowest temperature on this thermometer is -4° F (-20° C), the lowest possible temperature (called absolute zero) is about -459° F (-273° C). This temperature occurs only when atoms and molecules have no kinetic energy, or motion, at all. Fahrenheit (F) and Celsius (C) are the most commonly used scales of temperature.

Calcium oxide, also known as quicklime

Enough energy is released to boil some of the water

The lid prevents too much heat from escaping through the top

Ice is packed into these two spaces

The hot object is placed in the basket

STUDYING HEAT

Scottish chemist Joseph Black carried out many crucial experiments with heat. He measured the amount of heat needed to raise the temperature of different substances by one degree. He believed this was related to how much heat fluid each substance could hold, so he called it "heat capacity." We now know that heat is not a fluid, but scientists still use Black's term today.

A CAPACITY FOR MELTING ICE

French scientists Antoine Lavoisier (1743–94) and Pierre-Simon Laplace (1749–1827) invented the "ice calorimeter"—an instrument that could measure the heat capacity (see right) of different substances. A hot object placed in the basket would melt ice that is packed around it. The temperature of ice remains constant as it melts. Once the object has cooled down to the same temperature as the ice, the melted ice would be weighed and, from this, the heat capacity of the object could be worked out. Lavoisier believed that heat was a fluid and even considered it as a chemical element, to which he gave the name "caloric."

Cutaway section reveals how a calorimeter works

Melted ice runs out through this pipe

GENERATING HEAT BY FRICTION

Benjamin Thompson (1753–1814) was born in Massachusetts and was given the title Count Rumford after working for the Bavarian government. While watching the boring of cannon barrels in a Munich weapons factory, he noticed that huge amounts of heat were generated by friction between the cutting tools and the metal gun barrels. If heat were a fluid, it would have been used up very quickly, but the heat generated by friction continued to be released as long as the barrels were drilled. In the 1790s, Count Rumford concluded that heat must be a form of motion.

THE LINK BETWEEN FRICTION AND HEAT

When things are rubbed, they become hot. The 19th-century equipment shown here demonstrates that there is a link between mechanical "work" (kinetic energy, pp. 16–17) and heat. Water in the small copper tube heats up from the friction that occurs between the revolving copper tube and the wood as the handle is turned. The more it is turned, the hotter the water becomes—it could even be boiled.

The temperature of the water in the tube can be measured with a thermometer

Handle is rapidly turned, rotating the wheel

Friction occurs when the wood and copper tube rub together

Electromagnetism

ELECTRICITY AND MAGNETISM have been known for about 3,000 years. It was noticed long ago that when some materials are rubbed, they can attract or repel other objects. Quite separately, people noticed that some natural materials seemed to have unusual powers that attracted objects with iron in them. During the 18th century, experimenters were familiar with most of the ways in which electricity and magnetism could behave. But the two were seen as separate. Each one was thought to be carried by a "fluid" (pp. 18–19) that passed between materials, causing the attractions and repulsions people had observed. In the first half of the 19th century an amazing discovery was made—electricity can make magnetism, and magnetism can make electricity. The discoveries of electromagnetism were very important to an understanding of energy. If these two "natural forces" could change from one to the other, maybe other "forces of nature" could do so, too. The stage was set for the development of the Law of Conservation of Energy (pp. 24–25).

MICHAEL FARADAY
One of the most important figures in the development of an understanding of electromagnetism was Englishman Michael Faraday (1791–1867). He explored the relationship between electricity and magnetism by careful and inspired experiment at the Royal Institution in London, England.

Magnetism

The strange, invisible forces of magnetism had puzzled people from the time magnetic rocks were discovered. What makes a compass needle move? How does a magnet know when a nearby object contains iron? Even when scientists began to study magnetism, there seemed to be no connection between this "natural force" and the other "forces of nature," as they were called, such as light, gravity, heat, and electricity.

The pins are pulled to the stone by a magnetic force

LEADING THE WAY
Early people found that magnetic rocks like this would always point in the same direction if suspended on a string, making them useful to travelers for finding directions. They were named "lodestones," meaning "leading stones."

MAGNETIC COMPASS
The Earth acts as a huge magnet, for reasons which are still not fully understood. Because compasses contain magnets that are able to move freely, they respond to the Earth's magnetic field. This is an early mariners's compass. The magnet is beneath the card.

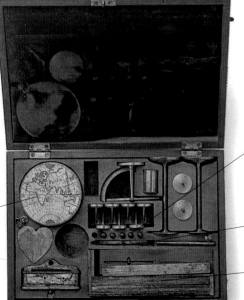

Spheres made of magnetite, a magnetic iron ore

Magnetic model of the Earth

Compass needle

EXPERIMENTER'S BOX
This beautiful box from the 18th century is full of objects used to experiment with magnetism. It shows that people were fascinated by the effects of magnetism and tried to find out more about them. The first person to describe fully the various effects of magnetism was Dr. William Gilbert (1544–1603) in his book *De Magnete*. He also tried to explain the attraction of the planets to the Sun in terms of magnetism.

Bar magnets

Electricity

Although electricity was known to the ancient Greeks, the scientific study of electricity was only really begun in the 16th century by William Gilbert. He discovered, for example, that objects "charged" with electricity either attracted (pulled) or repelled (pushed away) other "charged" objects. Electricity was studied with great interest. Many theories were put forward to explain it, and how it caused objects to move, and even made sparks (pp. 18–19). Scientists soon began to search for a connection between these effects and other "forces of nature."

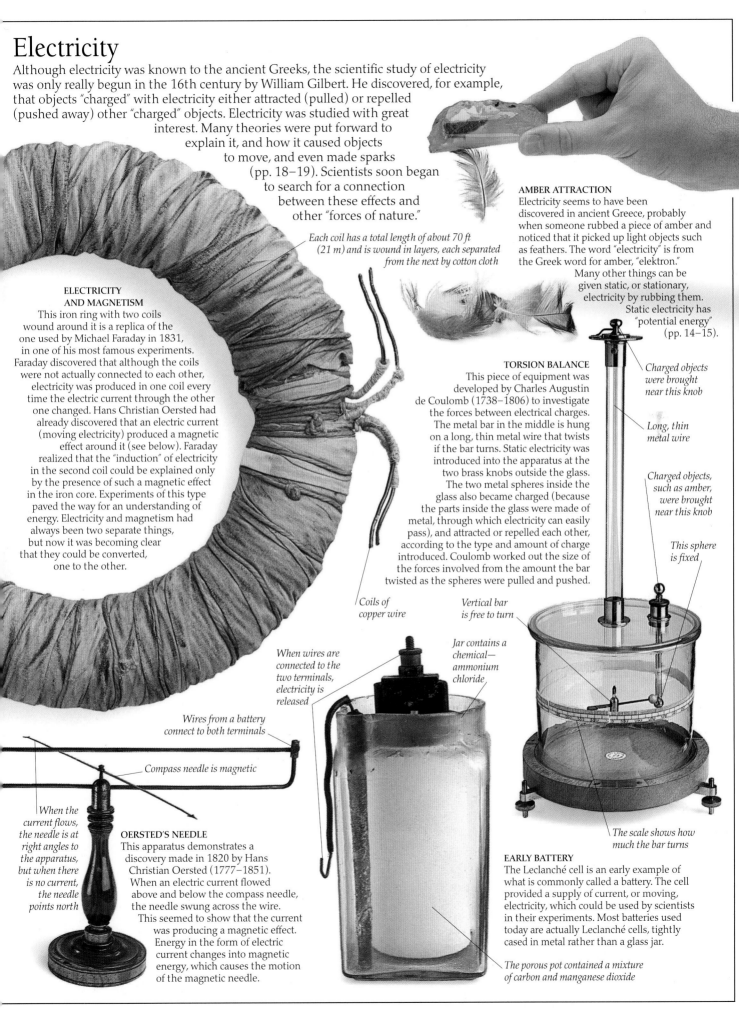

Each coil has a total length of about 70 ft (21 m) and is wound in layers, each separated from the next by cotton cloth

ELECTRICITY AND MAGNETISM

This iron ring with two coils wound around it is a replica of the one used by Michael Faraday in 1831, in one of his most famous experiments. Faraday discovered that although the coils were not actually connected to each other, electricity was produced in one coil every time the electric current through the other one changed. Hans Christian Oersted had already discovered that an electric current (moving electricity) produced a magnetic effect around it (see below). Faraday realized that the "induction" of electricity in the second coil could be explained only by the presence of such a magnetic effect in the iron core. Experiments of this type paved the way for an understanding of energy. Electricity and magnetism had always been two separate things, but now it was becoming clear that they could be converted, one to the other.

AMBER ATTRACTION

Electricity seems to have been discovered in ancient Greece, probably when someone rubbed a piece of amber and noticed that it picked up light objects such as feathers. The word "electricity" is from the Greek word for amber, "elektron." Many other things can be given static, or stationary, electricity by rubbing them. Static electricity has "potential energy" (pp. 14–15).

Charged objects were brought near this knob

Long, thin metal wire

TORSION BALANCE

This piece of equipment was developed by Charles Augustin de Coulomb (1738–1806) to investigate the forces between electrical charges. The metal bar in the middle is hung on a long, thin metal wire that twists if the bar turns. Static electricity was introduced into the apparatus at the two brass knobs outside the glass. The two metal spheres inside the glass also became charged (because the parts inside the glass were made of metal, through which electricity can easily pass), and attracted or repelled each other, according to the type and amount of charge introduced. Coulomb worked out the size of the forces involved from the amount the bar twisted as the spheres were pulled and pushed.

Charged objects, such as amber, were brought near this knob

This sphere is fixed

Coils of copper wire

Vertical bar is free to turn

Jar contains a chemical— ammonium chloride

When wires are connected to the two terminals, electricity is released

Wires from a battery connect to both terminals

Compass needle is magnetic

When the current flows, the needle is at right angles to the apparatus, but when there is no current, the needle points north

OERSTED'S NEEDLE

This apparatus demonstrates a discovery made in 1820 by Hans Christian Oersted (1777–1851). When an electric current flowed above and below the compass needle, the needle swung across the wire. This seemed to show that the current was producing a magnetic effect. Energy in the form of electric current changes into magnetic energy, which causes the motion of the magnetic needle.

The scale shows how much the bar turns

EARLY BATTERY

The Leclanché cell is an early example of what is commonly called a battery. The cell provided a supply of current, or moving, electricity, which could be used by scientists in their experiments. Most batteries used today are actually Leclanché cells, tightly cased in metal rather than a glass jar.

The porous pot contained a mixture of carbon and manganese dioxide

The conservation of energy

BY THE 1840S IT HAD BECOME APPARENT that the "forces of nature," which had been thought of as separate "imponderable fluids" (pp. 18–19), could be transformed into each other. For example, the work of Oersted and Faraday (pp. 22–23) showed that electricity and magnetism can change from one to the other. Mechanical "work," such as lifting a weight, can be converted to heat by friction (pp. 20–21). It was the painstaking work of the amateur scientist James Joule (1818–89) that began to prove that "energy," as it became known, cannot be created or destroyed, it can only change in form. This idea is known as the conservation of energy.

NATURAL FORCES
In 1847 German scientist Hermann von Helmholtz (1821–94) became the first person to explain the conservation of energy clearly. He said that all natural forces are either "living" (kinetic energy, pp. 16–17) or "tensional" (potential energy, pp. 14–15) and can be converted into one another. The word energy did not take on its current scientific meaning until the mid 19th century.

As the handle is turned, the small electromagnet spins

The whole box is placed in the middle of a huge electromagnet

Gearing transfers kinetic energy from the handle to electromagnet

JAMES PRESCOTT JOULE
The son of a wealthy English brewer, Joule converted a room in his father's house into a laboratory. In 1838 he began his measurements of heat given out by various processes. Legend has it that he even spent much of his honeymoon studying a waterfall, to see if the water heated up slightly as it splashed into a pool at the bottom. The unit of energy, the joule (pp. 36–37), was named after him.

JOULE'S REVOLVING ELECTROMAGNET
In the early part of the 1840s Joule wanted to show that the electrical energy generated by mechanical energy in a dynamo can produce another form of energy, heat. He built a small revolving electromagnet, which was turned rapidly between the poles of another electromagnet that surrounded the box shown here. He enclosed the revolving electromagnet in a glass tube full of water and measured the temperature of the water before and after the experiment to within 1/30 of a degree Fahrenheit (1/50 Celsius). As the electromagnet spun it generated an electric current, which could be measured by a sensitive meter. Joule found that the current warmed the water. The amount of heat produced was always directly related to the electric current, which was in turn directly related to the amount of mechanical work used to turn the handle.

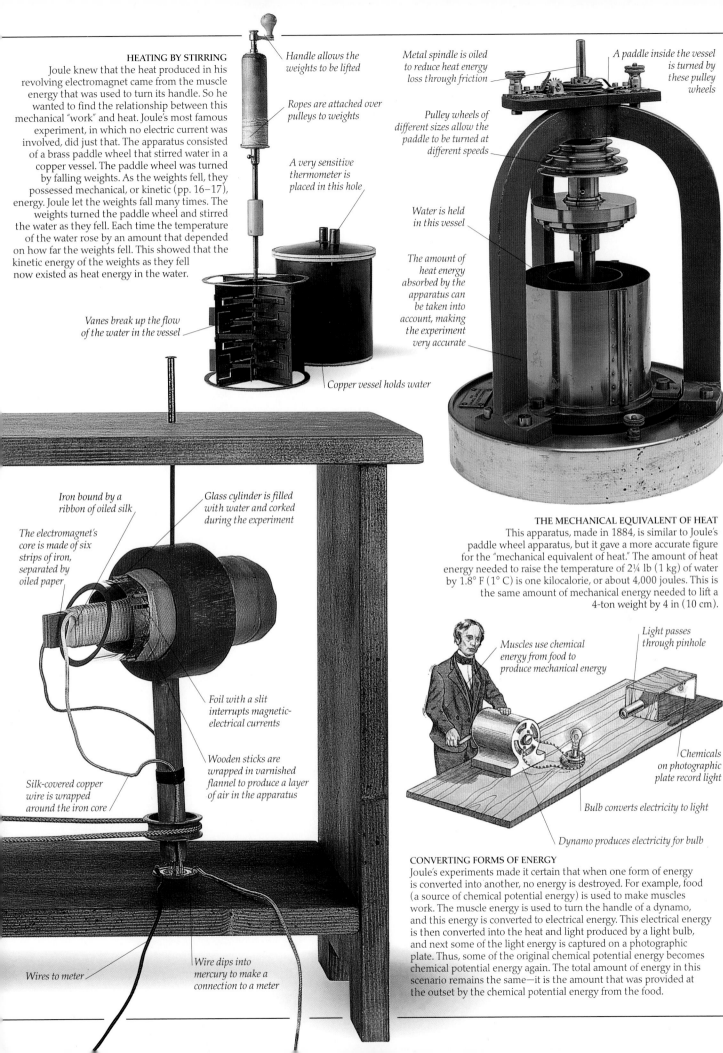

HEATING BY STIRRING

Joule knew that the heat produced in his revolving electromagnet came from the muscle energy that was used to turn its handle. So he wanted to find the relationship between this mechanical "work" and heat. Joule's most famous experiment, in which no electric current was involved, did just that. The apparatus consisted of a brass paddle wheel that stirred water in a copper vessel. The paddle wheel was turned by falling weights. As the weights fell, they possessed mechanical, or kinetic (pp. 16–17), energy. Joule let the weights fall many times. The weights turned the paddle wheel and stirred the water as they fell. Each time the temperature of the water rose by an amount that depended on how far the weights fell. This showed that the kinetic energy of the weights as they fell now existed as heat energy in the water.

Handle allows the weights to be lifted

Ropes are attached over pulleys to weights

A very sensitive thermometer is placed in this hole

Vanes break up the flow of the water in the vessel

Copper vessel holds water

Metal spindle is oiled to reduce heat energy loss through friction

A paddle inside the vessel is turned by these pulley wheels

Pulley wheels of different sizes allow the paddle to be turned at different speeds

Water is held in this vessel

The amount of heat energy absorbed by the apparatus can be taken into account, making the experiment very accurate

THE MECHANICAL EQUIVALENT OF HEAT

This apparatus, made in 1884, is similar to Joule's paddle wheel apparatus, but it gave a more accurate figure for the "mechanical equivalent of heat." The amount of heat energy needed to raise the temperature of 2¼ lb (1 kg) of water by 1.8° F (1° C) is one kilocalorie, or about 4,000 joules. This is the same amount of mechanical energy needed to lift a 4-ton weight by 4 in (10 cm).

Iron bound by a ribbon of oiled silk

Glass cylinder is filled with water and corked during the experiment

The electromagnet's core is made of six strips of iron, separated by oiled paper

Foil with a slit interrupts magnetic-electrical currents

Wooden sticks are wrapped in varnished flannel to produce a layer of air in the apparatus

Silk-covered copper wire is wrapped around the iron core

Wires to meter

Wire dips into mercury to make a connection to a meter

Muscles use chemical energy from food to produce mechanical energy

Light passes through pinhole

Chemicals on photographic plate record light

Bulb converts electricity to light

Dynamo produces electricity for bulb

CONVERTING FORMS OF ENERGY

Joule's experiments made it certain that when one form of energy is converted into another, no energy is destroyed. For example, food (a source of chemical potential energy) is used to make muscles work. The muscle energy is used to turn the handle of a dynamo, and this energy is converted to electrical energy. This electrical energy is then converted into the heat and light produced by a light bulb, and next some of the light energy is captured on a photographic plate. Thus, some of the original chemical potential energy becomes chemical potential energy again. The total amount of energy in this scenario remains the same—it is the amount that was provided at the outset by the chemical potential energy from the food.

Thermodynamics

HEAT BEHAVES IN A PREDICTABLE WAY. For example, when ice is placed in hot water, it melts. Heat—and other forms of energy—acts as if it obeys "laws" that restrict its behavior, and the study of heat as a form of energy is called thermodynamics. The "laws of thermodynamics" were worked out during the mid 19th century. The "law of conservation of energy" (pp. 24–25) says that energy cannot be created or destroyed, but can only change from one form to another. This is the first law of thermodynamics. Any form of energy can be converted entirely into heat. But when heat energy is changed into other forms, it can never do so entirely. Some of it always remains as heat, and temperatures always even out. This is the second law of thermodynamics. The behavior of heat energy can be explained by the fact that it is the motion of particles of matter—atoms and molecules. The temperature of matter is the average energy of all its particles. Conduction, the transfer of heat between matter in contact, happens because the particles of a hot object transfer some of their energy to those of a cooler object.

COOL BOTTLE
This bottle from Sudan was designed to keep drinks cold on hot days. To work, the bottle itself must be wet. Water on the side of the bottle evaporates, and this requires energy. The energy is supplied by the bottle and its contents in the form of heat. As they lose heat, they become cooler. This is what happens to a person when they are wet on a hot day and that is why they feel cold.

FOREVER IN MOTION
No machine can ever be 100 percent efficient because a certain amount of energy will always be lost as heat. This means that there can be no such thing as a perpetual motion machine, which would work for ever and never run out of energy, but many people still try to make one. This attempt was built in 1747. Iron balls fell on to a large wheel and turned the wheel around to operate the diagonal screw. The screw would then lift the balls up to repeat the process perpetually. But in practice the machine did not work because it would eventually slow down to a halt as its energy was lost as heat.

AN INTELLIGENT BOTTLE?
A variation of the vacuum flask invented by Dewar (above right) was mass-produced in the early 20th century and sold under the trade name Thermos. Because they keep hot drinks hot and cold drinks cold, they are useful for picnics, as this 1940s advertisement shows. The flasks cannot tell the difference between temperatures, but their internal vacuum stops conduction, so the temperature of the liquid does not change.

Liquid is put into flask through top opening

Top of the flask is closed to prevent convection

STOPPING THE ESCAPE OF HEAT
The vacuum flask, or Dewar flask, was invented by the Scottish physicist James Dewar (1842–1923). This is one of Dewar's experimental flasks that has been cut away to reveal the inside. The flask contains a partial vacuum between its walls that greatly reduces conduction, the transfer of heat energy between matter in contact. A perfect vacuum contains no matter so does not conduct heat. Heat energy can become radiation (pp. 40–41) and can pass between particles, even in a vacuum, but the vacuum flask has silvered walls that reflect radiated heat. The flask is closed to maintain the vacuum and prevent convection, the transfer of heat by air circulation.

Air is taken out through this tube to create a vacuum

Vacuum between the inner and outer walls prevents conduction

Liquid is kept inside

Silvered walls reflect radiated heat

Water
pipe

Thermometers
measure the
temperature of
the cooling
water

Air is pumped
in here

HOW TO MAKE AIR LIQUID

Air is a mixture of gases. If gases are cooled enough, they
become liquids. One way of doing this is by forcing them
to expand suddenly. This is what happens in a Hampson
air liquifier. Air is pumped in at the top under pressure. It is
forced through the tiny nozzle at the bottom,
and as it leaves the nozzle it expands into
an almost empty space. This expansion
requires energy, which has to come from
within the gas, so the gas cools. The
cooling effect is large enough to make
some of the air change to a liquid
form. The rest of the air is pumped
around again to repeat the process.

Pipes carry water to
cool the pressurized
gas, which heats up
as it is pressurized

Dial gives
measurement
of pressure

Insulation
prevents heat from
outside warming
the liquid gas

Pipe brings cold
air back to the top

Water
circulates here

The glass cover
prevents breezes
from turning
the vanes

Vanes turn when
electromagnetic
radiation falls
on them

One side of each
aluminum vane is coated
with mica, which absorbs
more of the radiation

Air molecules
typically travel
at many
hundreds of
mph (kph)

TURNING THE VANES

There are millions and millions of air
molecules inside the glass cover of this Crookes's
radiometer. They are all moving around randomly,
bouncing into each other, the vanes, and the glass.
One side of each vane gets hotter than the other
side because it is coated with mica, which absorbs
more electromagnetic radiation (pp. 40–41), such as
light, than aluminum, which is reflective. This
warms the surrounding air, which further
increases the speed of the molecules. They
bump into the vane more often on the
warm side, pushing it around.

4

FREEZING HOT

When ice is placed into a hot liquid, the ice will melt
and become liquid, and the liquid will cool. But why
does the liquid not solidify to become ice? Because heat
energy passes from hot to cold, eventually evening out.
This is the second law of thermodynamics. As the ice
cubes in the glass melt with the heat energy from
the hot water, the water will become cooler. This will
continue until the mixture is at the same temperature
throughout. It is possible to make heat energy pass from
cold objects to hot, but to do so energy needs to be
supplied; for example, in a refrigerator it is supplied by
the energy used in running the refrigeration process.

Pressurized air is forced through nozzle

PARTICLES OF ICE AND LIQUID

Thinking of matter in terms of its particles helps to
explain why ice cubes melt in hot water. The
water molecules that make up an ice cube have less kinetic
energy (pp. 16–17) than those of the hot water, and
merely vibrate around a fixed position. Hot water
molecules have more kinetic energy and move
around randomly. Sometimes they bump into
molecules at the edge of the ice cube and transfer
some of their kinetic energy to them. This transfer of
kinetic energy then continues until the energy is shared
between all the molecules in the mixture. The molecules
in the ice are given enough kinetic energy to break free of
each other, and they become liquid water. The hot water
molecules slow down as they lose some of their energy,
which means that they will become cooler. Eventually,
the whole mixture will become the same temperature.

Liquid
collects
here

Liquid is
drained
off here

Ice cube   Hot water

Ice molecules have too
little energy to break free

Hot water
molecules move
randomly, bumping
into each other

Steam energy

THE FIRST USE OF STEAM POWER was to drive pumps that drew water from flooded mines. English inventor Thomas Newcomen (1663–1729) installed the first practical steam engine at a mine in Dudley, UK, in 1712. Inside his machine was a piston that moved up and down inside a large cylinder. This piston was attached to a pump. The engines were popular but inefficient, because they needed huge amounts of coal to function. In 1765, Scottish engineer James Watt (1736–1819) made more efficient steam engines. At the same time, he introduced gearing that changed the up-and-down motion of the piston into a rotational one that could drive machines in factories. In the early 19th century, inventors began designing engines that used steam at high pressure. Those engines were small and powerful enough to drive locomotives (pp. 30–31).

Large tank contains water

Wooden beam rocks as the piston moves up and down

Chain is connected to the piston

Rod controls taps

Cylinder contains a piston that moves up and down

Water is sprayed into the cylinder to condense the steam

Taps allow steam and water into and out of cylinder

Coal is put through this spout on to a grate inside

The burned coal falls on to this tray

MINERS FRIEND
Thomas Savery (1650–1715) patented the design for this steam pump in 1698. The pump was intended to clear water from flooded mines, but the pipes carrying the steam often burst.

As the steam escapes here, the ball rotates

The steam is forced through the pipes and into the ball

HERO'S AEOLIPILE
This is a model of an aeolipile, invented by a Greek engineer, Hero of Alexandria (c. 100 CE). It was a forerunner of Parsons's steam turbine (pp. 32–33). Water in the boiler gained heat energy from a fire underneath. As the water boiled, steam was formed and forced out through the holes in the arms of the ball. The ball turned as a "reaction" to the escape of steam, so this is a "reaction turbine." The machine was not powerful enough to do any useful work.

Water is placed in the boiler and heated

A fire provides the heat energy to boil water in the boiler

EXPERIMENTS WITH STEAM
Willem 's Gravesand (pp. 16–17) used this small copper sphere in his experiments with gases. The sphere contained water, which was heated to boiling point over a fire. The sphere was then fixed to the wheels, and a hole in the sphere was opened. The force of the escaping steam pushed the sphere forward.

A ROYAL DEMONSTRATION
This small steam engine was made by or for John Theophilus Desaguliers (1683–1744) around 1740 to demonstrate the principles of the "atmospheric" steam engine to the British royal family. An atmospheric engine creates a near vacuum, usually beneath a piston, so that the air pressure on the other side can push the piston. This is the same way that a drinking straw works, except that instead of sucking air out to create the vacuum, steam from a boiler is "condensed" to form water in a cylinder, leaving mostly empty space. The air above the piston pushes with the force of atmospheric pressure. The energy is actually transferred to the piston from the millions of air molecules that hit the top of the piston each second (pp. 26–27). This model used steam energy to pump water from a bucket on the floor to the box halfway up.

SPRAYING COLD WATER

Thomas Newcomen's steam engine (see right) was an atmospheric engine that pumped water from the bottom of a mine at the rate of 525 gallons (2,000 liters) per minute. The steam condensed inside the cylinder when cold water was sprayed into it. This was inefficient, because heat was wasted as the cylinder cooled. James Watt improved this by making the steam condense away from the cylinder, so the cylinder was kept hot.

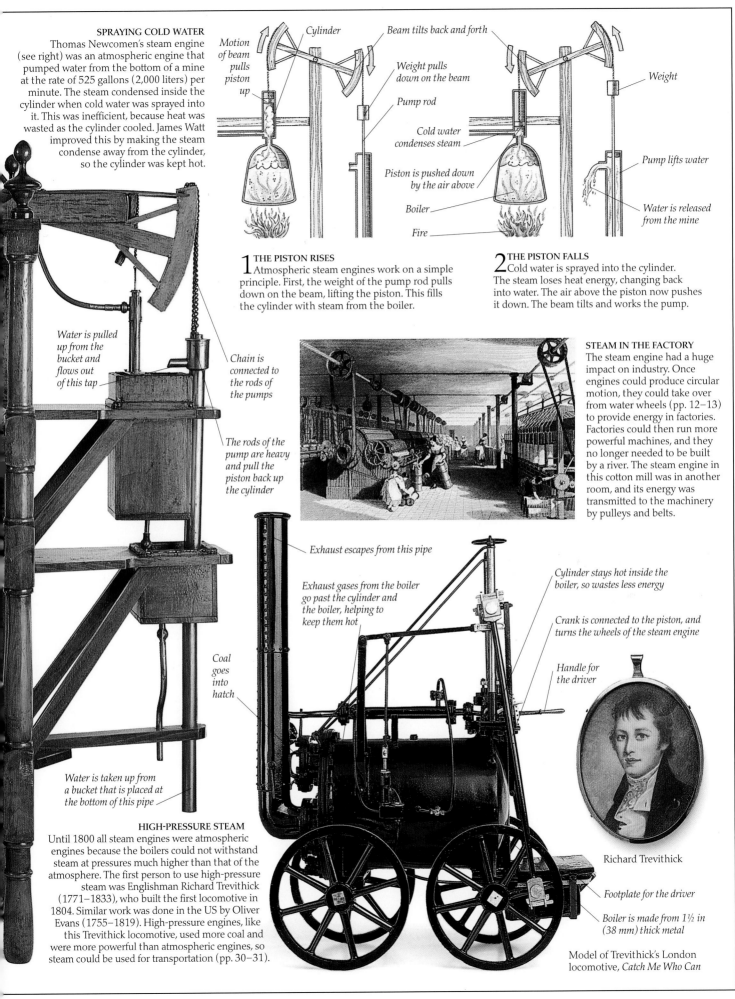

Motion of beam pulls piston up

Cylinder

Beam tilts back and forth

Weight pulls down on the beam

Pump rod

Cold water condenses steam

Piston is pushed down by the air above

Boiler

Fire

Weight

Pump lifts water

Water is released from the mine

1 THE PISTON RISES
Atmospheric steam engines work on a simple principle. First, the weight of the pump rod pulls down on the beam, lifting the piston. This fills the cylinder with steam from the boiler.

2 THE PISTON FALLS
Cold water is sprayed into the cylinder. The steam loses heat energy, changing back into water. The air above the piston now pushes it down. The beam tilts and works the pump.

Water is pulled up from the bucket and flows out of this tap

Chain is connected to the rods of the pumps

The rods of the pump are heavy and pull the piston back up the cylinder

STEAM IN THE FACTORY
The steam engine had a huge impact on industry. Once engines could produce circular motion, they could take over from water wheels (pp. 12–13) to provide energy in factories. Factories could then run more powerful machines, and they no longer needed to be built by a river. The steam engine in this cotton mill was in another room, and its energy was transmitted to the machinery by pulleys and belts.

Exhaust escapes from this pipe

Exhaust gases from the boiler go past the cylinder and the boiler, helping to keep them hot

Cylinder stays hot inside the boiler, so wastes less energy

Crank is connected to the piston, and turns the wheels of the steam engine

Handle for the driver

Coal goes into hatch

Water is taken up from a bucket that is placed at the bottom of this pipe

Richard Trevithick

Footplate for the driver

Boiler is made from 1½ in (38 mm) thick metal

HIGH-PRESSURE STEAM
Until 1800 all steam engines were atmospheric engines because the boilers could not withstand steam at pressures much higher than that of the atmosphere. The first person to use high-pressure steam was Englishman Richard Trevithick (1771–1833), who built the first locomotive in 1804. Similar work was done in the US by Oliver Evans (1755–1819). High-pressure engines, like this Trevithick locomotive, used more coal and were more powerful than atmospheric engines, so steam could be used for transportation (pp. 30–31).

Model of Trevithick's London locomotive, *Catch Me Who Can*

Energy for transportation

MOVING PEOPLE AND GOODS from place to place is a vital part of any civilization. The earliest ways of getting around made use of animals (pp. 8–9) and wind (pp. 12–13) as energy sources. Toward the end of the 18th century the first canals were built—with horses providing the energy to drag barges along canals. However, everyday travel on land was still slow and awkward. At the beginning of the 19th century the steam engine (pp. 28–29) became powerful enough to be given wheels and take its energy source of coal with it. The railroad age had begun, and soon trains were carrying passengers and freight in many countries. By the end of the 19th century the internal combustion engine had been invented. It made use of the energy released by rapidly burning fuel inside its cylinders, making motor vehicles possible. As technology improved in the 20th century, other forms of transportation appeared, such as streetcars, aircraft, and the space shuttle.

ONE HORSEPOWER
The horse has always been an important source of energy for transportation. Assyrian horse-drawn chariots like this were very fast and used in races and for hunting. Groups of horses were used for transportation in other ways. Stagecoaches often used 12 horses to pull them. In 1783, James Watt defined the power of one horse as a unit of power, the "horsepower."

Steering wheel

Oak frame

Driver's seat

Horizontal cylinder

Passenger seat

Brake

The engine ran on gas

Belts transmit energy to the wheels

ENERGY CARRIAGE
The internal combustion engine is compact and powerful enough for its energy source—usually gasoline—to be carried with it. This is a model of a motor carriage made in 1875 by Siegfried Marcus, an Austrian engineer. The car had a top speed of about 4 mph (6 kph). Although it worked remarkably well for its time, Marcus did not realize the potential of his automobile. It was another 11 years before the first real automobile appeared on the market. It was made by Karl Benz (1844–1929) of Germany.

MOVING STEAM ENGINES
Locomotives took over from stagecoaches and canals when people began to realize that they were faster and more powerful. The first passenger railroad opened in 1830 in the UK. There was much opposition to the railroads, mainly from the owners of canals and stagecoach companies. Many people were afraid of the railroads because they thought it was dangerous to travel at speeds greater than 12 mph (20 kph).

FOUR-CYLINDER ENGINE
This engine from a 1920s Austin Seven automobile is cut away to show inside one of the cylinders. The engine has four cylinders, each containing a piston that moves up and down about 2,400 times per minute. The piston's motion can be described by four movements, or strokes. First, the piston moves down, and gas vapor is sucked into the cylinder from the carburetor. Then the piston moves up again to compress the vapor at the top of the cylinder. This is the "compression stroke." Next, a spark from the spark plug causes the gas vapor to explode, forcing the piston down the cylinder again. This supplies the energy for the car. Finally, the piston moves back up, pushing the used fuel out to the exhaust pipe. This "four-stroke cycle" has been used in most automobiles made since 1876.

OTTO'S ENGINE
In 1876 Nikolaus Otto of Germany became the first person to build and sell a four-stroke engine—on which most later engines have been based. He called it the "Silent Otto" because it ran so quietly. One of the main features of the four-stroke engine is the "compression stroke." More energy is released if the fuel is a vapor under pressure. The idea was first developed by a Frenchman, Alphonse Beau de Rochas (1815–91), but it was Otto who made it a success.

Pulley wheel is connected to the dynamo

Camshaft sprocket connects crankshaft to camshaft

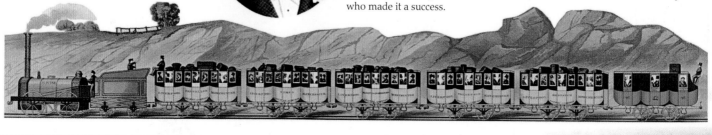

INNOVATIVE DEVELOPMENTS IN CITY TRANSPORTATION

This is a model of a streetcar (or trolley) that was part of a transportation service in London, UK, in the early 1900s. The first streetcars appeared in New York City in 1832. They were horse-drawn, but soon other energy sources were tried—first steam, then electricity. The first electric streetcars were introduced in Berlin, Germany, in 1881. They used electric rails in the road, which could be dangerous. As an alternative, overhead cables were developed. Electricity with high potential energy (pp. 14–15) was supplied through the wires, powering an electric motor in the streetcar that turned the wheels. Streetcars, like trains, must stay on rails. In a crowded city street this could be a problem, so streetcars were soon replaced in most places by other forms of transportation, such as buses. However, streetcars can help prevent traffic jams and are appearing in some cities again. They have the advantage of being less polluting than other forms of transportation.

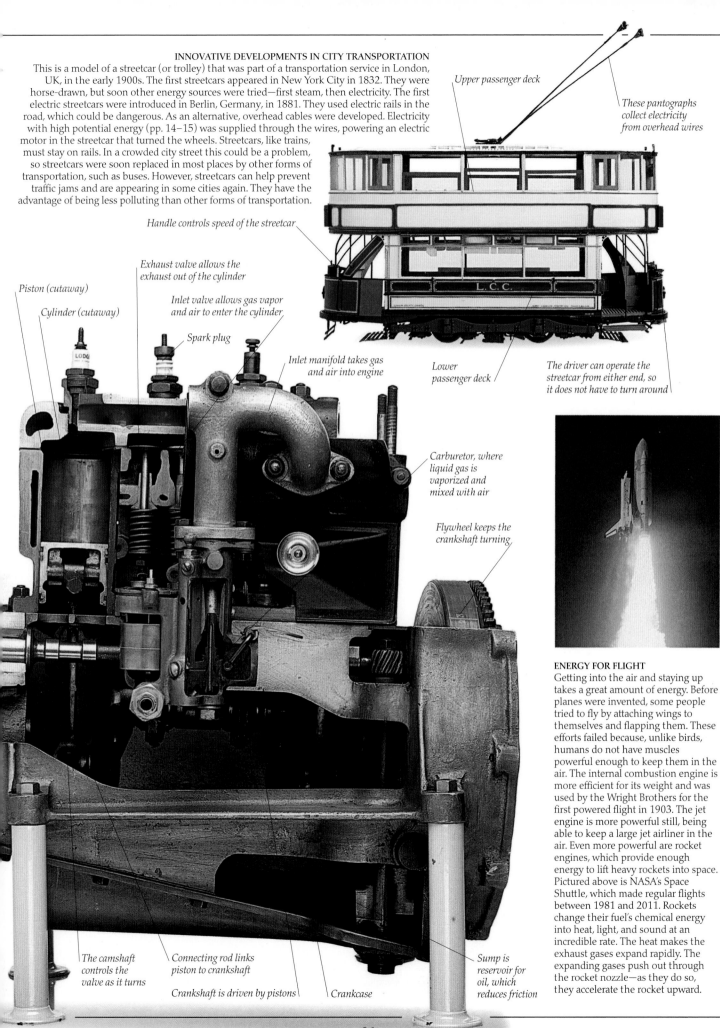

Upper passenger deck

These pantographs collect electricity from overhead wires

Handle controls speed of the streetcar

Exhaust valve allows the exhaust out of the cylinder

Piston (cutaway)

Cylinder (cutaway)

Inlet valve allows gas vapor and air to enter the cylinder

Spark plug

Inlet manifold takes gas and air into engine

Lower passenger deck

The driver can operate the streetcar from either end, so it does not have to turn around

Carburetor, where liquid gas is vaporized and mixed with air

Flywheel keeps the crankshaft turning

The camshaft controls the valve as it turns

Connecting rod links piston to crankshaft

Crankshaft is driven by pistons

Crankcase

Sump is reservoir for oil, which reduces friction

ENERGY FOR FLIGHT

Getting into the air and staying up takes a great amount of energy. Before planes were invented, some people tried to fly by attaching wings to themselves and flapping them. These efforts failed because, unlike birds, humans do not have muscles powerful enough to keep them in the air. The internal combustion engine is more efficient for its weight and was used by the Wright Brothers for the first powered flight in 1903. The jet engine is more powerful still, being able to keep a large jet airliner in the air. Even more powerful are rocket engines, which provide enough energy to lift heavy rockets into space. Pictured above is NASA's Space Shuttle, which made regular flights between 1981 and 2011. Rockets change their fuel's chemical energy into heat, light, and sound at an incredible rate. The heat makes the exhaust gases expand rapidly. The expanding gases push out through the rocket nozzle—as they do so, they accelerate the rocket upward.

Generating electricity

Electricity is the most convenient form of energy to use in the home and in many parts of industry. But electrical energy must be produced, or generated. There are many ways to generate a voltage, or electrical potential energy (pp. 14–15), but the best way is to use electromagnetism (pp. 22–23). Michael Faraday visualized a magnet's energy as a "field." When metal moves through a "magnetic field," a voltage is produced. Using this effect, various "magneto-electric" machines were developed, and by the end of the 19th century steam, engines (pp. 28–29) and wind and water turbines (pp. 58–59) were turning large generators to make electricity for homes, offices, and factories. One very important invention that enabled electricity to be generated on a large scale was the steam turbine. It was much faster and more efficient than the steam engines that had been used before. Steam turbines are still used to drive most generators.

GRAMME DYNAMO

A dynamo is a machine that turns mechanical energy (pp. 8–9) into electrical energy. Zénobe Théophile Gramme (1826–1901) of Belgium invented the first practical dynamo in 1870. This one produced "direct current," or d.c. Direct current flows in one direction only—today most generators produce alternating current, or a.c., which changes direction rapidly. The coils in the middle of the dynamo were turned at high speed by a steam engine, and the two large coils produced a magnetic field around them. This generated the electricity.

Sir Charles Parsons

STEAM TURBINE GENERATOR

Until the invention of the steam turbine in 1884, dynamos and generators were powered by traditional steam engines. But these were inefficient and could not turn fast enough to produce electricity on a large scale. The steam turbine was developed by the Irish engineer Sir Charles Parsons (1854–1931). The steam turbine here made use of the energy of high-pressure steam at 400° F (200° C) to drive the generator. The turbine turned 4,800 times every minute, and yet it ran so smoothly that it did not have to be bolted down. It generated 100,000 joules (pp. 36–37) of electrical energy every second (100 kW).

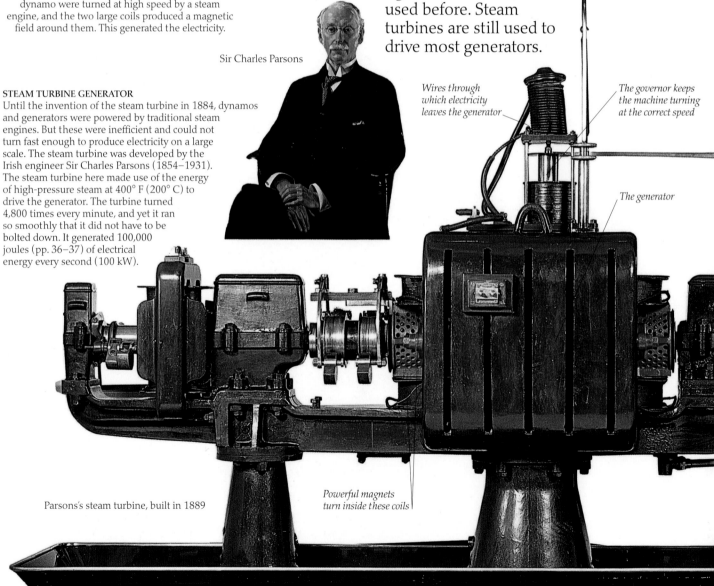

Wires through which electricity leaves the generator

The governor keeps the machine turning at the correct speed

The generator

Parsons's steam turbine, built in 1889

Powerful magnets turn inside these coils

EARLY POWER PLANT

By 1882, American inventor Thomas Edison was operating a power plant in New York City. The use of electricity soon spread to much of the world. This is a model of a power plant built at Deptford, in London, UK. It began generating electricity in 1889, and it was capable of supplying electrical energy at a rate of over one million joules every second. Designed by Sebastian Ziani de Ferranti (1864–1930), an engineer living in London, it was the largest and most powerful power plant of its time, providing energy for half of London. It was powered by a huge steam engine. All large power plants since the beginning of the 20th century have run either on steam turbines or water turbines. As electricity came to be supplied on a large scale, its energy could be used in an ever-increasing number of ways, in industry and in the home (pp. 34–35).

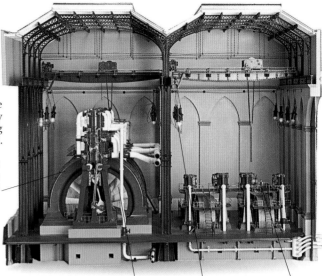

Huge "triple-expansion" steam engines made the most of the energy of steam by letting it expand in three stages

The steam to drive the engines was produced by burning coal in boilers in another part of the plant

Electric lighting

Notice how small a person is compared to the generators

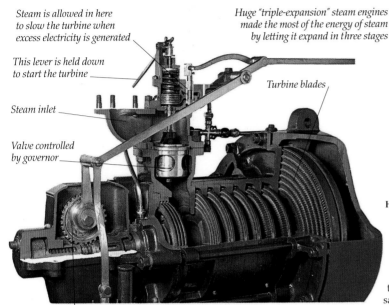

Steam is allowed in here to slow the turbine when excess electricity is generated

This lever is held down to start the turbine

Steam inlet

Valve controlled by governor

Turbine blades

This wheel rotates rapidly to prevent the valve from seizing up

HOW THE STEAM TURBINE WORKS

Steam entered at the top of Parsons's steam turbine and forced its way down, past the valve. It found its way into the axle of the turbine blades and then pushed its way out, turning the blades as it did so. As the steam finished in one blade, it went to the next. Each blade is slightly bigger than the next—this is because to get the energy from the steam, the steam must be allowed to expand. For the same reason, the steam outlet is bigger than the steam inlet.

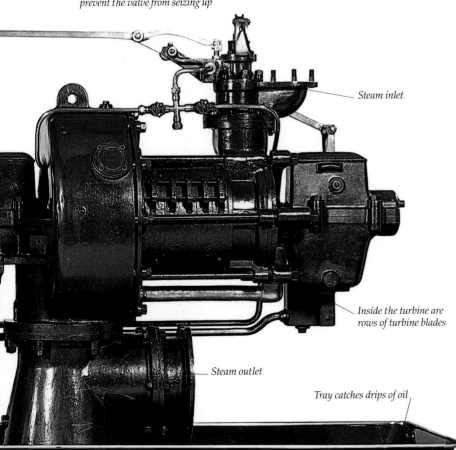

Steam inlet

Inside the turbine are rows of turbine blades

Steam outlet

Tray catches drips of oil

TOWERS AND TRANSFORMERS

To distribute electrical energy over large distances, it is transformed, or changed, to a high voltage (usually between 132,000 and 400,000 volts) before being transformed back to smaller voltages (240 volts). There are transformers at each end of the line—at the power plant and at local "substations." Alternating current is used (p. 32) because direct current cannot be transformed and does not travel well. The system for distributing electricity was devised by an Eastern European-born American electrical engineer Nikola Tesla (1856–1943). Towers carrying overhead cables are the most common way of distributing electricity, because digging power lines underground can be expensive. The large cooling towers are a familiar sight at power plants. They cool the water that is used to condense the steam that leaves the turbines, turning the steam back into water.

Energy in the home

For thousands of years people have used energy to cook their food and to provide heat and light in their homes. The energy was usually obtained from fire (pp. 10–11) by burning wood, oil, or candles. During the 19th century, coal gas (pp. 54–55) was used in millions of homes in many countries. Later, powerful electrical generators (pp. 32–33) were built to supply electricity to homes. Electricity is more convenient than gas as a source of energy in the home because it can be used for jobs other than heating, lighting, and cooking. It provides the energy for an ever-increasing variety of appliances such as hair driers, microwave ovens, and televisions.

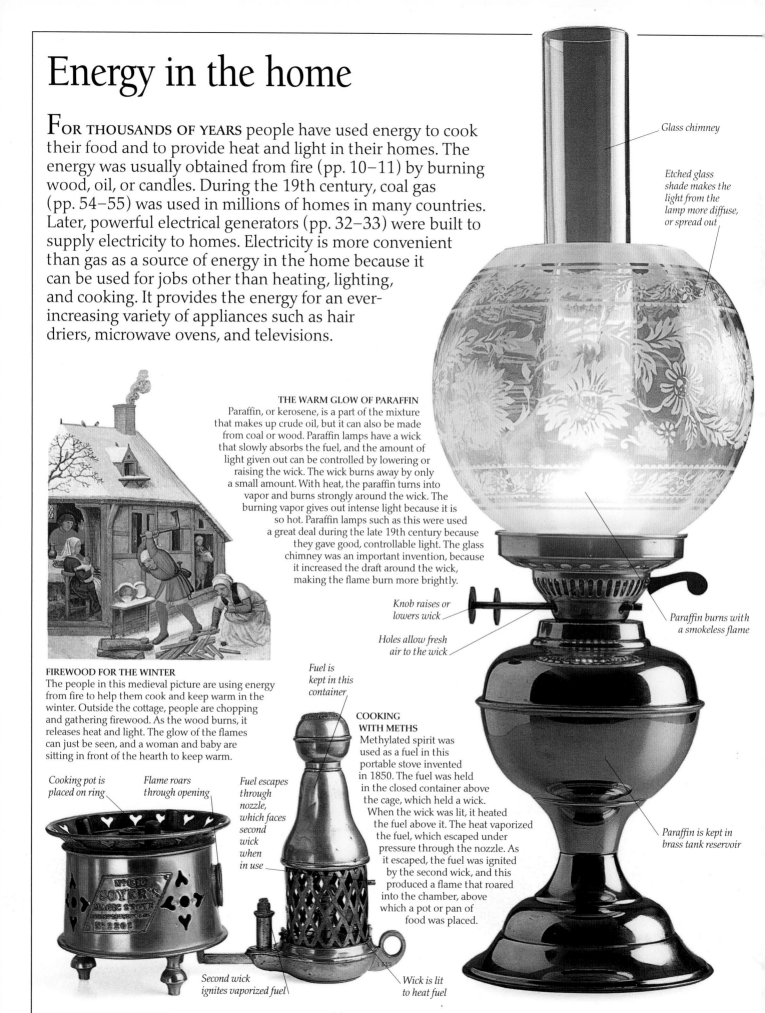

Glass chimney

Etched glass shade makes the light from the lamp more diffuse, or spread out

THE WARM GLOW OF PARAFFIN
Paraffin, or kerosene, is a part of the mixture that makes up crude oil, but it can also be made from coal or wood. Paraffin lamps have a wick that slowly absorbs the fuel, and the amount of light given out can be controlled by lowering or raising the wick. The wick burns away by only a small amount. With heat, the paraffin turns into vapor and burns strongly around the wick. The burning vapor gives out intense light because it is so hot. Paraffin lamps such as this were used a great deal during the late 19th century because they gave good, controllable light. The glass chimney was an important invention, because it increased the draft around the wick, making the flame burn more brightly.

Knob raises or lowers wick

Holes allow fresh air to the wick

Paraffin burns with a smokeless flame

FIREWOOD FOR THE WINTER
The people in this medieval picture are using energy from fire to help them cook and keep warm in the winter. Outside the cottage, people are chopping and gathering firewood. As the wood burns, it releases heat and light. The glow of the flames can just be seen, and a woman and baby are sitting in front of the hearth to keep warm.

Cooking pot is placed on ring

Flame roars through opening

Fuel is kept in this container

Fuel escapes through nozzle, which faces second wick when in use

COOKING WITH METHS
Methylated spirit was used as a fuel in this portable stove invented in 1850. The fuel was held in the closed container above the cage, which held a wick. When the wick was lit, it heated the fuel above it. The heat vaporized the fuel, which escaped under pressure through the nozzle. As it escaped, the fuel was ignited by the second wick, and this produced a flame that roared into the chamber, above which a pot or pan of food was placed.

Paraffin is kept in brass tank reservoir

Second wick ignites vaporized fuel

Wick is lit to heat fuel

BLOWING HOT AND COLD
A fan is just what is needed on a hot day. The blades of an electric fan are turned by an electric motor, but the blades of this unusual gas-powered fan of 1904 are turned in a very different way. Gas is burned in two cylinders at the base of the fan, like the cylinders of an internal combustion engine in a car (pp. 30–31). There is a piston in each of the cylinders that is pushed up as the gas explodes. The pistons are connected to the axle at the center of the fan blades, and the blades are made to turn as the pistons move up and down. Because this fan burns gas, the cooling effect it has is only slightly greater than the heat it produces.

Fan blades turn, creating a cooling breeze

Fan moves as the pistons move up and down

Rod connects piston to fan blades

Axle

Top of cylinder

Piston is inside here

Gas is let in through this pipe

Heavy cast-iron body ensures stability

ENERGY FOR BATHTIME
Hot water has not always been available in the home because heat is needed to raise the temperature of the water. Without inventions such as water boilers, like this 1925 gas-burning model, bath water must be heated on stoves or fires, or people must bathe in cold water.

BOILING THE KETTLE
Electric kettles heat water by passing electricity through a heating element. This one was made in the 1920s and has a heating element in its base, away from the water.

Wicker handle

Lid

Spout

Kettle is made of brass

Heating element is inside the base of the kettle

Electrical connections are made to these two terminals

ENERGY FOR ENTERTAINMENT
The introduction of electricity into the homes of millions of people across the world has increased the number of ways that energy is used. This television is hooked up to a satellite dish that can detect signals sent via satellite from anywhere in the world. The light and sound that make up the action of a television picture are coded into a radio wave (pp. 40–41) and sent to a satellite far above the Earth's surface. The satellites then amplify the signal and send it back to Earth, to be detected by satellite dishes and decoded into a television picture. The first event to have satellite coverage was the 1964 Olympic Games in Tokyo.

COOKING WITH RADIATION
Microwave ovens cook food by focusing intense electromagnetic radiation (pp. 40–41) on to food placed inside. The microwave radiation is matched to the frequency that makes hydrogen atoms, such as those in water, vibrate, so the water inside the food heats up.

Measuring energy

THERE ARE MANY SITUATIONS in which it is necessary to know how much energy is being changed from one form to another. For example, a company generating electricity needs some way to find out how much electrical energy is used by each of its customers. In most scientific experiments there is some form of energy measurement. A meter is an instrument that measures energy, and the standard unit of energy is the joule (J), named after James Joule (pp. 24–25). But energy can be measured in many different units. A calorie (pp. 52–53) is defined as the amount of heat energy (pp. 20–21) needed to raise the temperature of 1 kg of water by 1° C. Power is simply the rate at which the energy is changed. The watt (W) is the unit of power and is named after James Watt (pp. 28–29). One W means 1 J of energy being changed each second. So, a 1,000 W (1 kW) electrical appliance changes 1,000 J (1 kJ) of electrical energy into the same amount of heat energy each second. If the appliance was left on for one hour, it would use 3,600 kJ, or 1 kilowatt-hour (1 kWh), of electrical energy.

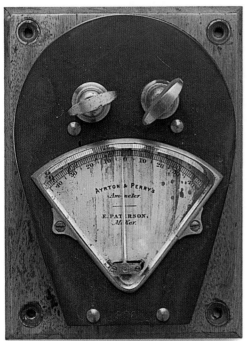

NATURAL ENERGY METERS
Human and animal brains receive signals from specialized nerve endings, which measure energy, or changes in energy. This picture shows the light-sensitive receptors of the eye, which measure the light energy that enters the eye. There are nerves that are sensitive to heat and pressure in the skin, to light in the eyes, and to vibrations in the ears. Without these energy sensors, humans and animals would have no way of sensing the world around them.

MOVING NEEDLE METER
Electricity is the most commonly used form of energy, and there are many ways of measuring it. When working with electric circuits, it is usually important to know how much electricity is being supplied (current), and how much energy each unit of electricity is able to supply (voltage). Most meters that measure electricity work by changing a little of the electrical energy into magnetism, and making the resulting magnetic force move a needle on a dial. This meter from the late 1800s was one of the first to measure current and voltage reliably.

Cutaway of electric current meter, or ammeter (side view)

Top view of an electric current meter, or ammeter

Electricity passes through these coils and produces magnetism

Small magnet is turned by the magnetism from the coils, causing the needle to move

Glass protects the needle from damage, and from air currents that can affect the measurement

Wires are connected to these terminals to complete the circuit

Coil produces a magnetic force that depends on the current flowing

Wires can be connected to these terminals

Moveable weight

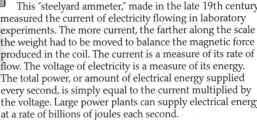

Scale

ELECTRICAL SCALES
This "steelyard ammeter," made in the late 19th century, measured the current of electricity flowing in laboratory experiments. The more current, the farther along the scale the weight had to be moved to balance the magnetic force produced in the coil. The current is a measure of its rate of flow. The voltage of electricity is a measure of its energy. The total power, or amount of electrical energy supplied every second, is simply equal to the current multiplied by the voltage. Large power plants can supply electrical energy at a rate of billions of joules each second.

BURNING FUEL
Different fuels can release different amounts of chemical energy as heat. This is methylated spirits, which is often used as a fuel for small stoves (pp. 34–35). Methylated spirits, butane, propane, and paraffin are all common domestic fuels. Gasoline, another common fuel, is used mainly in car engines (pp. 30–31). One liter of gas will release about 40 million J when burned completely. Depending on how it is burned, most of this will become heat immediately. This makes it a very convenient fuel to burn in engines.

ONE JOULE OF ENERGY
The international unit of energy is the joule. An apple weighing 100 g lifted 1 m is given 1 joule (1 J) of potential energy (pp. 14–15). If it is dropped through the same distance, that 1 J of potential energy will be changed to 1 J of kinetic energy (pp. 16–17) as it falls, and then to 1 J of heat and sound energy as it hits the ground. An 11-watt light bulb changes 11 J of electrical energy into light and heat every second. That is enough energy to lift 11 apples 1 m. The Sun (pp. 48–49) radiates 390 million billion billion J of energy into space every second.

THERMAL ENERGY
The molecules of any substance are in constant motion, so they possess kinetic energy (pp. 16–17). The temperature of a substance is related to the average kinetic energy of all of the particles of which it is made. A thermometer is an energy measuring device. The jam in this pot is at a temperature of 152° F (67° C). Each of the molecules of the jam has a tiny amount of kinetic energy. There are so many molecules that the total heat energy, or thermal energy, of the jam is about 58,000 J.

DRIVING A CAR
All the energy that a car uses to accelerate and keep moving comes from the gas or diesel it burns in its engine. A typical "fuel-efficient" car will use about 1½ gallons (6 liters) of fuel on a 60-mile (100-km) drive. This means that about 240 million J of energy is obtained from the fuel. Only about a third of the energy obtained from the fuel turns the wheels. Some cars can produce 100 "horsepower." One horsepower is about 746 W (746 J/sec), which is approximately the power that a horse can develop in pulling a load.

A MESSAGE IN SMOKE

Before the invention of the telegraph, long-distance communication was difficult. Smoke signals were one way to get a message beyond shouting distance, but they were useful for communicating only in clear daylight. They were used in many parts of the world, including China, Australia, and North America. At night, when smoke signals could not be seen, the light of fires was used to send messages. There were many other methods of long-distance communication that did not rely on electricity, such as beating logs and drums, or signaling with flags.

ALL FORMS OF COMMUNICATION require energy—both to create a message and to send it. One person waving to another, for example, needs energy to move their hand, then light energy transmits the image of the wave to the other person. Because of this need for energy, communicating over large distances was difficult before the use of electricity, which made communication much faster and easier. The first large-scale form of communication to use electricity was the telegraph. One of the first successful telegraphs was constructed in 1837. It consisted of compass needles that turned as a current flowed through a wire. Over the next century many more electrical machines were developed to aid communication. In 1876, the telephone was invented, and its use quickly spread across the world. By the early 20th century, radio waves (pp. 40–41) were being used to communicate over large distances. Since the 1930s, radio communication has become part of everyday life, and satellites have made worldwide communication faster and easier.

Insulated handle is pressed to send messages

When contact is made, the instrument is ready to receive

Wire connects from here to electromagnet to receive incoming messages

Wire connects from here to receiving station

Wire connects from here to a battery

Morse Key No. 1

MORSE AND HIS CODE

Samuel Morse (1791–1872) was an American artist and scientist who made important contributions to communication. In 1838 he put the Morse code into operation to send messages over long distances via the telegraph. The letters of the alphabet are each represented by a combination of short and long electrical pulses, called "dots" and "dashes," which are produced on transmitting machines. These pulses can be received in a number of ways. One of the most common is that they activate a sounder, a machine that converts the electrical pulse into long or short beeps. Shown above is an early Morse key, which is simply a switch that sends a dot or a dash when the handle is pressed. This one was used by the Post Office Telegraph service in the UK.

Samuel Morse

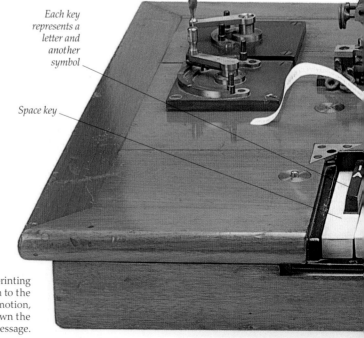

Each key represents a letter and another symbol

Space key

TAPPING OUT A MESSAGE

In the 1850s the Hughes Telegraph was used a great deal, mainly in France. It was invented by David Hughes of Kentucky. The printing wheel, which has the letters of the alphabet, prints a letter on to the printing paper when one of the 28 keys is pressed. In the same motion, electrical contact is made, and a pulse of electrical energy is sent down the telegraph line to an identical machine, which prints the same message.

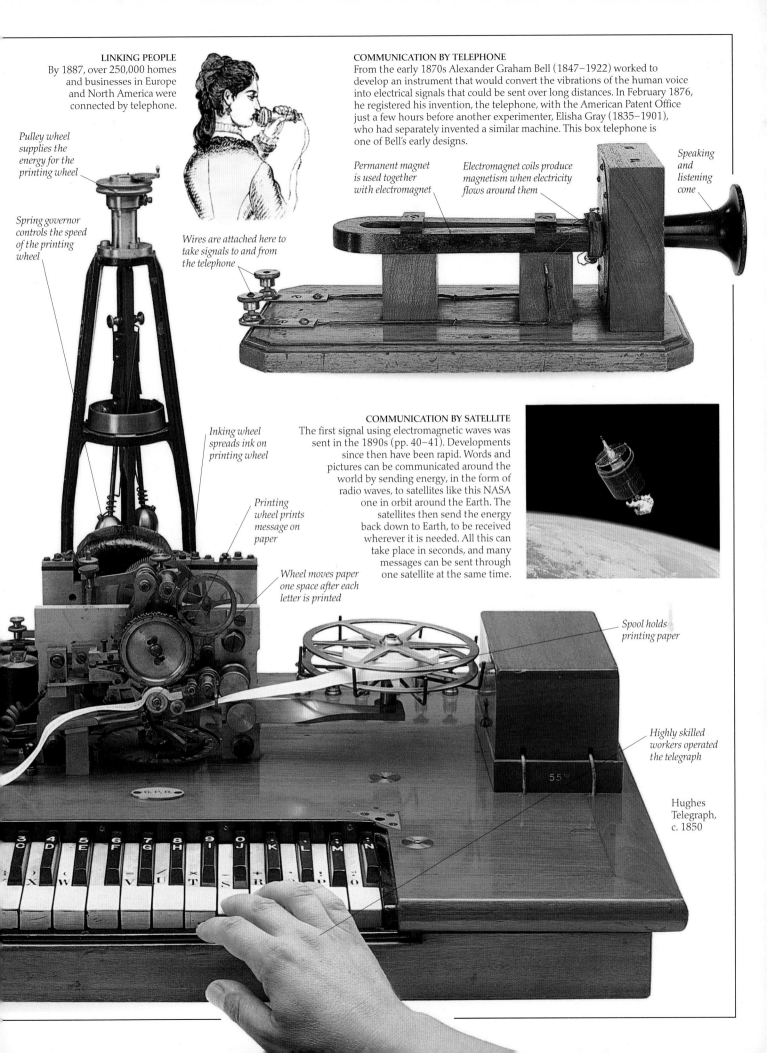

LINKING PEOPLE
By 1887, over 250,000 homes and businesses in Europe and North America were connected by telephone.

Pulley wheel supplies the energy for the printing wheel

Spring governor controls the speed of the printing wheel

Wires are attached here to take signals to and from the telephone

Inking wheel spreads ink on printing wheel

Printing wheel prints message on paper

Wheel moves paper one space after each letter is printed

COMMUNICATION BY TELEPHONE
From the early 1870s Alexander Graham Bell (1847–1922) worked to develop an instrument that would convert the vibrations of the human voice into electrical signals that could be sent over long distances. In February 1876, he registered his invention, the telephone, with the American Patent Office just a few hours before another experimenter, Elisha Gray (1835–1901), who had separately invented a similar machine. This box telephone is one of Bell's early designs.

Permanent magnet is used together with electromagnet

Electromagnet coils produce magnetism when electricity flows around them

Speaking and listening cone

COMMUNICATION BY SATELLITE
The first signal using electromagnetic waves was sent in the 1890s (pp. 40–41). Developments since then have been rapid. Words and pictures can be communicated around the world by sending energy, in the form of radio waves, to satellites like this NASA one in orbit around the Earth. The satellites then send the energy back down to Earth, to be received wherever it is needed. All this can take place in seconds, and many messages can be sent through one satellite at the same time.

Spool holds printing paper

Highly skilled workers operated the telegraph

Hughes Telegraph, c. 1850

Energy in waves

WHEN A PENDULUM SWINGS back and forth, or oscillates, it has a fixed amount of energy, which changes between potential energy at each end of its swing and kinetic energy at the center. The rate of oscillation is the frequency. An oscillating object can pass some or all of its energy on to other objects by a wave motion. For example, when water is forced to oscillate, the energy of the oscillation is spread out to the surrounding water by a wave as each water molecule affects its nearest neighbors. Sound travels in a similar way. In the 1860s, James Clerk Maxwell (1831–79) found that light waves are traveling oscillations of electromagnetic energy. He also predicted the existence of other electromagnetic waves, which were later demonstrated by Heinrich Hertz (p. 42).

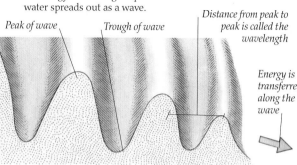

WATER RIPPLES
The energy of a falling drop of water spreads out as a wave.

Peak of wave   *Trough of wave*

Distance from peak to peak is called the wavelength

Energy is transferred along the wave

THE ANATOMY OF A WAVE
A cross-section of a water wave shows its structure. The peaks and troughs occur where water is displaced above or below the normal water level. The height of a peak is called the amplitude of the wave. Amplitude is reduced as the wave travels outward and the energy is spread over larger and larger circles. The water moves up and down, but not along with the wave—only the energy moves outward.

ELECTROMAGNETIC RADIATION
James Clerk Maxwell was a brilliant mathematician and physicist whose work on electromagnetism followed that of Michael Faraday (pp. 22–23). He put Faraday's discoveries into mathematical form, and his calculations suggested that light is an oscillation of energy between electricity and magnetism. His calculations also suggested that other types of electromagnetic waves exist with frequencies higher and lower than that of light. In 1888 the German physicist Heinrich Hertz (pp. 42–43) produced and detected lower-frequency electromagnetic waves in his laboratory, confirming Maxwell's ideas. These are now known as radio waves and are just part of the electromagnetic spectrum (pp. 42–43) that Maxwell had predicted.

LIGHT WAVE EXPERIMENT
This colorful demonstration, known as Newton's rings, suggests that light is a wave motion. This is because the colors are produced by "interference," an effect common to all waves. Two layers of glass are held together with screws, and both pieces reflect light from their surfaces. When two light waves combine, their peaks and troughs reinforce each other in some places and cancel each other out in others. When water waves interfere, the water can become choppy. In the same way, light interference causes bright and dark areas in this experiment.

Bright and dark patterns caused by interference

Screws adjust distance between two layers of glass

Prongs vibrate 440 times each second

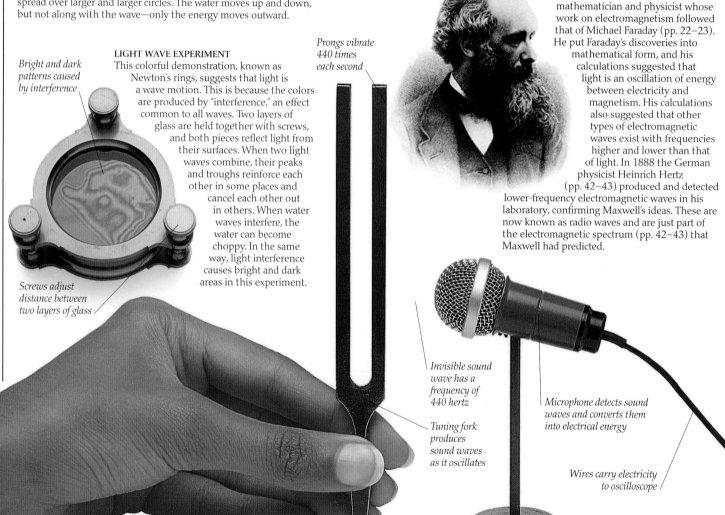

Invisible sound wave has a frequency of 440 hertz

Tuning fork produces sound waves as it oscillates

Microphone detects sound waves and converts them into electrical energy

Wires carry electricity to oscilloscope

RADIO WAVES FOR COMMUNICATION

Italian scientist Guglielmo Marconi (1874–1937) was a pioneer of radio communication. He realized that the electromagnetic waves Hertz had discovered could be used to transmit information. On December 11, 1901, Marconi transmitted a signal from Cornwall, England, to Newfoundland, Canada, a distance of about 2,000 miles (3,300 km). Radio soon proved to be a very effective method of communication. Since then, the energy of electromagnetic radiation has been used to carry huge amounts of information, including television pictures.

ENERGY THROUGH THE AIRWAVES

The logo of the RKO broadcasting company shows a radio transmitter sending out its radio waves in every direction.

TRACING THE ENERGY OF SOUND WAVES

When a tuning fork is struck, it oscillates at a definite frequency and disturbs the air at the same frequency. The energy of the disturbance spreads through the air as a sound wave, part of which meets the microphone. In the microphone the energy of the sound makes a coil of wire oscillate, again at the same frequency. A magnet sits in the middle of the coil of wire, and a small electric current is generated in the coil. Because the coil is moved back and forth, the current changes direction with the same frequency, passing as a wave down the wires to the oscilloscope. The oscilloscope, an instrument commonly used for testing electric circuits, displays the oscillating current on its screen.

Screen is coated with phosphorus, which glows when hit by electrons

Shape of sound wave is traced by an oscillating beam of electrons in the oscilloscope

Energy in packets

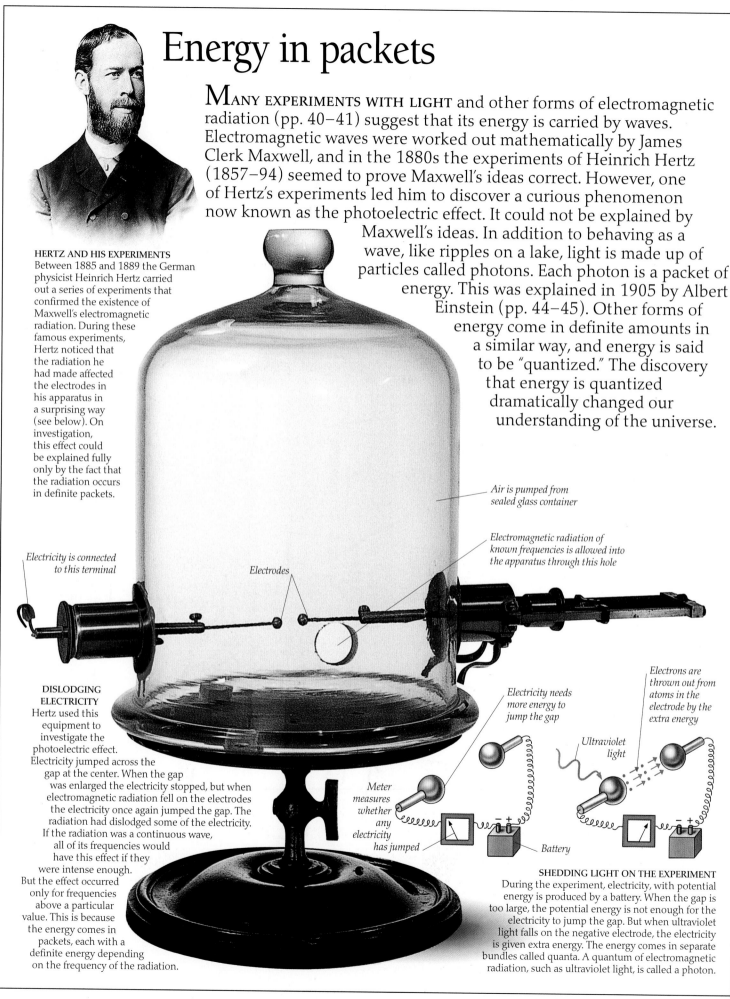

MANY EXPERIMENTS WITH LIGHT and other forms of electromagnetic radiation (pp. 40–41) suggest that its energy is carried by waves. Electromagnetic waves were worked out mathematically by James Clerk Maxwell, and in the 1880s the experiments of Heinrich Hertz (1857–94) seemed to prove Maxwell's ideas correct. However, one of Hertz's experiments led him to discover a curious phenomenon now known as the photoelectric effect. It could not be explained by Maxwell's ideas. In addition to behaving as a wave, like ripples on a lake, light is made up of particles called photons. Each photon is a packet of energy. This was explained in 1905 by Albert Einstein (pp. 44–45). Other forms of energy come in definite amounts in a similar way, and energy is said to be "quantized." The discovery that energy is quantized dramatically changed our understanding of the universe.

HERTZ AND HIS EXPERIMENTS
Between 1885 and 1889 the German physicist Heinrich Hertz carried out a series of experiments that confirmed the existence of Maxwell's electromagnetic radiation. During these famous experiments, Hertz noticed that the radiation he had made affected the electrodes in his apparatus in a surprising way (see below). On investigation, this effect could be explained fully only by the fact that the radiation occurs in definite packets.

Air is pumped from sealed glass container

Electromagnetic radiation of known frequencies is allowed into the apparatus through this hole

Electricity is connected to this terminal

Electrodes

DISLODGING ELECTRICITY
Hertz used this equipment to investigate the photoelectric effect. Electricity jumped across the gap at the center. When the gap was enlarged the electricity stopped, but when electromagnetic radiation fell on the electrodes the electricity once again jumped the gap. The radiation had dislodged some of the electricity. If the radiation was a continuous wave, all of its frequencies would have this effect if they were intense enough. But the effect occurred only for frequencies above a particular value. This is because the energy comes in packets, each with a definite energy depending on the frequency of the radiation.

Electricity needs more energy to jump the gap

Electrons are thrown out from atoms in the electrode by the extra energy

Ultraviolet light

Meter measures whether any electricity has jumped

Battery

SHEDDING LIGHT ON THE EXPERIMENT
During the experiment, electricity, with potential energy is produced by a battery. When the gap is too large, the potential energy is not enough for the electricity to jump the gap. But when ultraviolet light falls on the negative electrode, the electricity is given extra energy. The energy comes in separate bundles called quanta. A quantum of electromagnetic radiation, such as ultraviolet light, is called a photon.

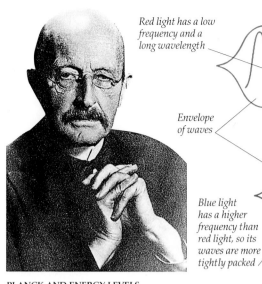

Red light has a low frequency and a long wavelength

Envelope of waves

Blue light has a higher frequency than red light, so its waves are more tightly packed

A PHOTON OF RED LIGHT
A photon does not really look like anything, but many people find it useful to think of it as a packet of waves because electromagnetic radiation behaves as waves and particles. The energy of a photon depends only on its frequency.

A PHOTON OF BLUE LIGHT
The frequency of blue light is higher than that of red light, so a blue wave packet would contain more tightly packed waves. The energy of a photon of blue light is about 0.0000000000000000005 joules; about twice as much as a photon of red light.

LIGHT SPECTRUM
White light is just a small portion of the complete spectrum of electromagnetic radiation. All such radiation is identical, except that the photons differ in the energy they carry. Photons of X-rays carry much more energy than those of white light, and photons of radio waves have much less energy than those of white light.
Prisms separate electromagnetic radiation according to the amount of energy and can be used to analyze the radiation from a hot object.

White light is made of a spectrum of colors

PLANCK AND ENERGY LEVELS
In the 1890s, Max Planck was studying the problem of radiation given off by hot objects. This had been a problem for some time because Maxwell's theory of electromagnetic waves could not explain the radiation from hot objects. In 1900, Planck made a bold suggestion. Instead of being allowed any amount of energy as they vibrated, the atoms of matter could have only particular values of energy. So, instead of losing energy continuously as they cool, atoms jump from one energy of vibration down to the next, giving out a definite amount of energy each time. This energy must come in separate packets, or photons. In 1905, Einstein developed this idea to explain the photoelectric effect.

LIGHT FROM SHOOTING STARS
Although they look white, these very hot shooting stars are actually giving off the whole spectrum of visible light, and more. The amount of each frequency present depends on the temperature of the shooting star. This can be explained only by the fact that the radiation comes in packets. The energy of each packet depends on its frequency.

Light-sensitive metal such as selenium is exposed to light

Photographer works out exposure times from the meter reading

Ammeter built into light meter registers electric current

SMETHURST HIGH-LIGHT AVO EXPOSURE METER

EXPOSURE

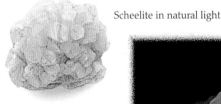

Scheelite in natural light

SHINING ROCKS
Many substances, such as this scheelite, fluoresce under ultraviolet light. This happens when photons of radiation with higher frequency (so higher energy) than visible light fall on them. This gives their atoms more energy. The atoms release this energy again, often in the form of lower-energy photons. These lower-energy photons are often those of visible light. This is one way substances can be made to glow in the dark.

A HELP TO PHOTOGRAPHERS
Light meters, such as this early one, became available in the 1930s. They use the photoelectric effect to measure the intensity of light. The metals in the meter are specially chosen because they are light sensitive, or affected by visible light. Photons of light hit the metal atoms and give up all their energy to electrons, dislodging them from the metal atoms. The electrons can then be measured by a meter that detects current. The brighter the light, the more electrons dislodged, and the greater the current.

Scheelite in ultraviolet light

Mass energy

By the end of the 19th century, scientists thought that the concept of energy was well understood. In 1905, Albert Einstein (1879–1955) challenged the accepted view of the world. During that year, he wrote four very important articles. One of these explained the photoelectric effect (pp. 42–43), and one involved heat energy (pp. 20–21). The most famous article discussed his Special Theory of Relativity, in which he discussed the fact that the speed of light is fixed. This fact led to some startling conclusions about space, time, and energy. In his fourth paper, he explored what Special Relativity could tell us about energy. Einstein discovered that energy has mass—and that mass is actually a form of energy. His celebrated equation, $E=mc^2$, describes this mass-energy idea mathematically. The E stands for a change in energy, c is the speed of light, and m is the corresponding mass. According to this, when 1 metric ton is lifted through 1 m, it gains 0.0000000001 g (0.000000000004 oz). This change in mass is so small that it becomes measurable only when huge amounts of energy are involved, such as in nuclear reactions (pp. 46–47).

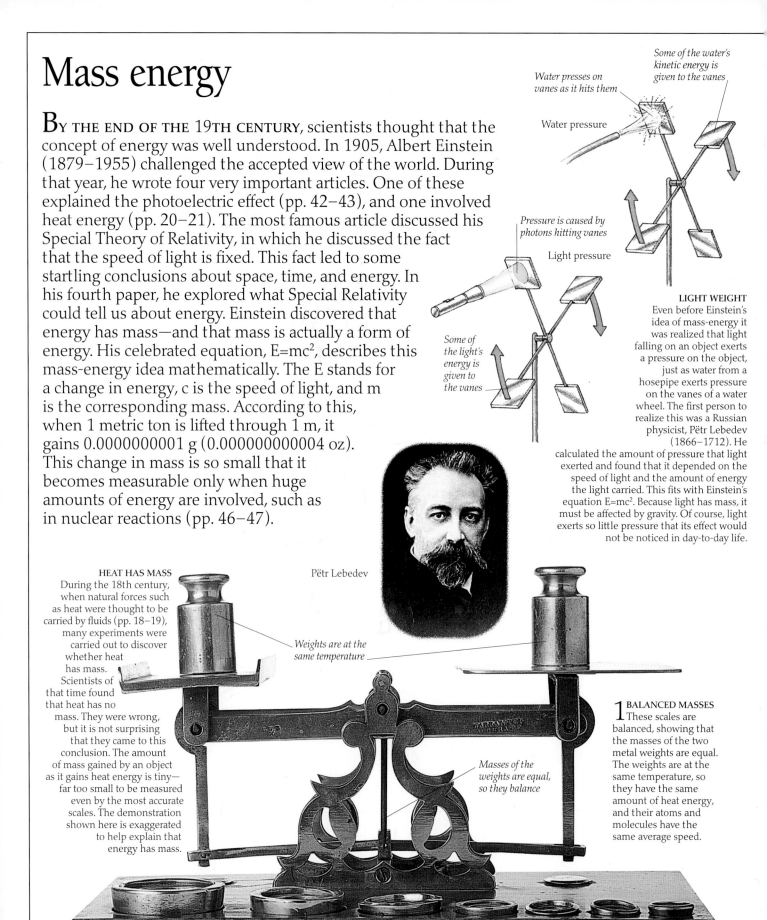

Water presses on vanes as it hits them

Some of the water's kinetic energy is given to the vanes

Water pressure

Pressure is caused by photons hitting vanes

Light pressure

Some of the light's energy is given to the vanes

LIGHT WEIGHT
Even before Einstein's idea of mass-energy it was realized that light falling on an object exerts a pressure on the object, just as water from a hosepipe exerts pressure on the vanes of a water wheel. The first person to realize this was a Russian physicist, Pëtr Lebedev (1866–1712). He calculated the amount of pressure that light exerted and found that it depended on the speed of light and the amount of energy the light carried. This fits with Einstein's equation $E=mc^2$. Because light has mass, it must be affected by gravity. Of course, light exerts so little pressure that its effect would not be noticed in day-to-day life.

Pëtr Lebedev

HEAT HAS MASS
During the 18th century, when natural forces such as heat were thought to be carried by fluids (pp. 18–19), many experiments were carried out to discover whether heat has mass. Scientists of that time found that heat has no mass. They were wrong, but it is not surprising that they came to this conclusion. The amount of mass gained by an object as it gains heat energy is tiny— far too small to be measured even by the most accurate scales. The demonstration shown here is exaggerated to help explain that energy has mass.

Weights are at the same temperature

1 BALANCED MASSES
These scales are balanced, showing that the masses of the two metal weights are equal. The weights are at the same temperature, so they have the same amount of heat energy, and their atoms and molecules have the same average speed.

Masses of the weights are equal, so they balance

EINSTEIN AND RELATIVITY

The German physicist Albert Einstein was born the year that James Clerk Maxwell (pp. 40–41) died. Although he did not do well at school, Einstein was a genius who was to change the face of science. Before Einstein, energy was energy and mass was mass. But Einstein's Special Theory of Relativity, first published in his article, "Does the Inertia of a Body Depend Upon its Energy Content?," suggested that energy and mass are directly linked. The truth of Einstein's insight has since been proved many times. He won a Nobel Prize in 1921 for his service to physics.

Metal weight gains heat energy from the flame

Tarnishing is caused by oxygen combining with the metal

Bunsen burner provides heat energy

MAKING MATTER

This colorful picture shows the trails left by tiny particles in the reaction chamber of a large particle accelerator, a machine used to produce nuclear reactions. Energy, in the form of two photons of electromagnetic radiation, enters at the right-hand side. Each one suddenly becomes matter in the form of an electron (green) and a positron (red). The electrons and positrons are electrically charged and spiral in the chamber's strong magnetic field. The long green line is another electron that has been knocked off an atom.

2 ADDING ENERGY, ADDING MASS

One of the metal weights from the scales is taken away and heated by a Bunsen burner. As the metal weight heats up, it gains heat energy. This increases the average speed of its atoms and molecules. It also increases the metal weight's mass, because energy has mass.

FASTER THAN THE SPEED OF LIGHT

Ever since the discovery that light travels at 186,000 mps (300,000 kps), people have dreamed of traveling at the same speed or faster. In the television series "Star Trek," the spaceship *Starship Enterprise* frequently travels faster than the speed of light. This is not really possible, because the speed of light is the speed limit in the universe. The faster an object travels, the more kinetic energy, and mass, it gains. At light speed, an object would become so heavy that an infinite amount of energy would be needed to move it.

Cool weight is unchanged

3 ENERGY IMBALANCE

When the metal weight is placed back on the scale, it no longer balances with the other weight. This is because it contains extra energy in the form of heat. In this demonstration the scales have been tipped to suggest an increase in mass, although in reality the increase is so small it could not be detected in this way.

Metal weight that was heated has gained heat energy, so it has also gained mass

Scales no longer balance

Energy from the nucleus

FERMI'S REACTION
On December 2, 1942, the first artificial nuclear chain reaction was produced by a team of scientists led by the brilliant Italian physicist Enrico Fermi (1901–54). The successful experiment took place in a squash court at the University of Chicago. A chain reaction works a bit like lighting a match. The heat from the friction of striking the match allows some of the atoms to burn, releasing more heat, which keeps the reaction going.

FROM THE EARLY 1900s scientists knew that the atoms that make up matter consist of tiny nuclei surrounded by electrons. The nucleus was found to be made up of tightly packed particles, which were named protons and neutrons. Electrons are held in the atom by electromagnetism (pp. 22–23), but the forces that hold the nucleus together are far greater. Those forces are the key to nuclear power. There are two main ways by which this energy can be released—fission and fusion. In each case a reaction occurs in the nuclei of atoms, and the matter left after the reaction has a little less mass than before. The "lost" mass is changed into energy (pp. 44–45), some of which is released as high-energy electromagnetic radiation (pp. 40–41). The rest becomes heat (pp. 20–21), which can be used to destroy things, in nuclear weapons, or to generate electricity, in nuclear reactors.

BALANCING THE REACTIONS
It is possible to measure the masses of the particles involved in a nuclear reaction. One common fission reaction involves a nucleus of uranium splitting into nuclei of barium and krypton. The reaction begins when one neutron bombards the uranium. During the reaction three neutrons are released. When the mass of the uranium nucleus before the reaction is compared to the mass of the barium and krypton afterward, it is found that some mass has disappeared. The missing mass has been converted into energy. In this example the mass lost is less than one thousandth of the mass present at the beginning of the reaction, and it is converted into just $\frac{1}{30,000,000,000,000}$ joule (J) for each atom of uranium. However, atoms are so small that if 1 kg of uranium was completely "fissioned" in this way, more than 10 million million J of energy would be released.

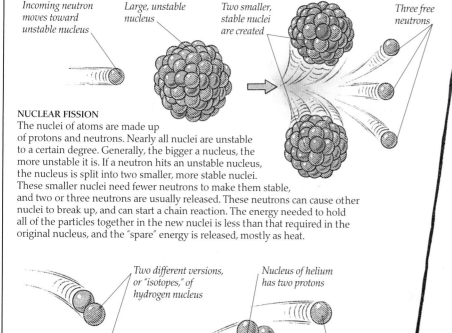

Incoming neutron moves toward unstable nucleus

Large, unstable nucleus

Two smaller, stable nuclei are created

Three free neutrons

NUCLEAR FISSION
The nuclei of atoms are made up of protons and neutrons. Nearly all nuclei are unstable to a certain degree. Generally, the bigger a nucleus, the more unstable it is. If a neutron hits an unstable nucleus, the nucleus is split into two smaller, more stable nuclei. These smaller nuclei need fewer neutrons to make them stable, and two or three neutrons are usually released. These neutrons can cause other nuclei to break up, and can start a chain reaction. The energy needed to hold all of the particles together in the new nuclei is less than that required in the original nucleus, and the "spare" energy is released, mostly as heat.

Two different versions, or "isotopes," of hydrogen nucleus

Nucleus of helium has two protons

Free neutron

NUCLEAR FUSION
At very high temperatures, small nuclei can be fused together to make larger ones. This is what happens at the heart of stars such as the Sun (pp. 48–49). If the new nucleus needs less energy to hold it together than the old ones, energy will be released and mass will be "lost." The most common fusion reaction is the one that builds a nucleus of helium from nuclei of hydrogen. This reaction has been carried out in special fusion reactors, and many people hope that it will be the energy source of the future. It would be clean, safe, and there would be no radioactive waste.

Free neutron to bombard uranium nucleus

Uranium nucleus

HOW BIG IS A NUCLEUS?
There are a staggering 10,000 million million million molecules of sugar in this cube. Each molecule consists of 24 atoms. But most of an atom, and of the sugar cube, is empty space. This is because the nucleus of an atom takes up only one 1,000-million-millionth of the space of the atom. If a nucleus were the size of a sugar cube, an atom would be about half a mile (1 km) across.

TESTING THE HYDROGEN BOMB AT BIKINI

In 1939, the great physicist Albert Einstein sent a letter to US President Franklin D. Roosevelt. Einstein suggested that a nuclear chain reaction could be used to generate electricity, or to make a bomb. Einstein thought that a bomb would never actually be used, but instead would act as a "deterrent" in World War II. However, Einstein's suggestions were investigated, and since then many countries have acquired nuclear weapons. This explosion of hydrogen bomb was a test carried out on the Bikini Atoll in the Pacific Ocean in 1956. Hydrogen bombs use uncontrolled nuclear fusion to release huge amounts of energy. Atom bombs use nuclear fission.

a

Soil fused to the side of the bowl

Different parts of the soil took different forms

Rice bowl from Hiroshima

THE EFFECTS OF A NUCLEAR WEAPON

The first atomic bomb explosion was over Hiroshima, Japan, in World War II. It killed 80,000 people immediately, and another 60,000 died within a year from radiation sickness, which results from changes in living cells due to radiation from nuclear explosions. Atomic bombs release intense heat, great enough to fuse soil to the side of this rice bowl.

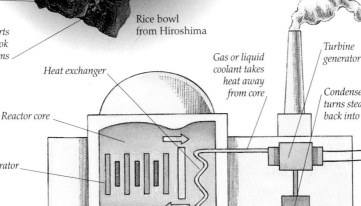

Steam is released from the cooling tower

Turbine generator

Gas or liquid coolant takes heat away from core

Condenser turns steam back into water

Electricity travels down wires to be distributed

Heat exchanger

Reactor core

Moderator

GENERATING ELECTRICITY WITH NUCLEAR ENERGY

Using fission, energy from the nucleus can be used to generate electricity. All nuclear power plants have a reactor core, a heat exchanger, and turbines. The core is where the nuclear reactions take place. In a reactor core, nuclear reactions are carefully controlled by the insertion of materials called "moderators," which absorb free neutrons that would otherwise increase the rate of the chain reaction. The heat exchanger takes heat from the core to a supply of water. The water is turned into high-pressure steam, and the steam drives the turbine generator to produce electricity.

Three "spare" neutrons

Barium nucleus

Krypton nucleus

Mass has been lost in the reaction, so the right-hand pan weighs less than the left-hand pan

THE IDEAL ENERGY SOURCE?

Nuclear power plants release no dangerous fumes during normal operation. However, after fission occurs, the "spent" fuel stays dangerously radioactive for thousands of years and must be buried deep underground or at sea. At this nuclear waste dump in Washington state, a Geiger counter is being used to monitor the radiation being released. Another problem with nuclear power is the danger of accidents. These can have devastating local and worldwide effects, like the disasters at Chernobyl in the Ukraine (p. 57), Three Mile Island in the US, and Windscale in the UK.

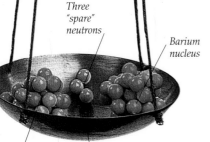

Energy from the Sun

THE SUN HAS ALWAYS been of great importance to people, providing heat and light. But early people could not have known the importance of the Sun as the provider of practically all the energy the Earth receives. Without the energy that reaches the Earth through space, there would be no plant or animal life on the planet. The energy of most alternative energy sources (pp. 58–59), such as wind energy, originally comes from the Sun. It is also the Sun's energy, stored in plants millions of years ago, that is released when fossil fuels (pp. 54–55) are burned. The Earth receives only a tiny fraction of the huge amount of energy released by the Sun. This energy comes from fusion reactions (pp. 46–47) deep at its center. The Sun emits such vast amounts of energy, which has mass (pp. 46–47), that it is losing millions of tons every second.

BASKING IN THE SUN
Reptiles such as this sand lizard are cold-blooded. This means they cannot regulate their body temperature. Many cold-blooded creatures react to changes in temperature by becoming more or less active. This shows how important the Sun's heating effect is to such animals. The sand lizard relies on the energy it gets directly from the Sun to warm its body.

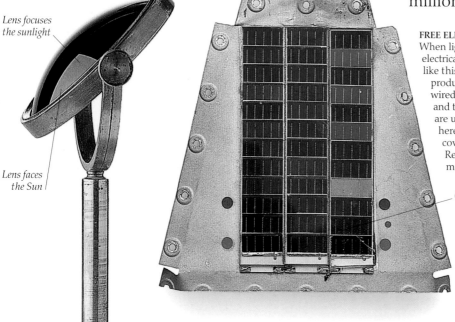

Lens focuses the sunlight

Lens faces the Sun

Metal stand for lens

FREE ELECTRICITY FROM THE SUN
When light hits the special chemicals in a solar cell, electrical potential energy, or voltage, is produced. A cell like this one from the communications satellite *Telstar* will produce only a small voltage, but a large number of cells wired together provides all the energy needed to receive and transmit signals from and to the ground. Solar cells are used as an alternative energy source (pp. 58–59) here on Earth, too. Many people have large panels covered with solar cells attached to their roofs. Researchers in many countries are finding ways to make solar cells ever cheaper and more effective.

Cells contain crystals of silicon, which convert solar energy into electricity

SUNLIGHT AND SUN HEAT
A convex lens such as this burning lens can focus sunlight to a point, causing paper to burn. The Sun radiates a range of frequencies in addition to visible light. Infrared is electromagnetic radiation (pp. 40–41) just outside the visible range. Although it cannot be seen by human eyes, its effects can often be felt as heat. The frequencies of infrared match those that start atoms and molecules vibrating. This means they heat up, and their heat can be enough to start a reaction. Burning lenses were often used by chemists to help reactions to happen.

Paper is scorched where sunlight shines

A FUSION OF IDEAS
In 1938, the German physicist Hans Bethe (b. 1906) first suggested that nuclear fusion (pp. 46–47) might be what provides the energy of stars such as the Sun. He was correct, but a better understanding of the processes involved has been the result of work by many great scientists. Bethe was rewarded for his discoveries in 1967 with the Nobel Prize for Physics.

LOOKING INSIDE THE SUN

The Sun is made up of a number of layers. The conditions in each layer are quite different. At the very center is the intensely hot core, where most of the energy of the Sun is produced. The energy is released by fusion (pp. 46–47). For fusion to take place, a very high temperature is required. The temperature in the core of the Sun is known to be about 27,000,000° F (15,000,000° C). The diameter of the Sun is about 3 billion times the width of this book, and its own gravity crams everything together at its center, causing huge pressures that result in heat being generated. Once started, the fusion reactions themselves release heat, which helps them to keep going. The energy released at the core travels outward from atom to atom, first by radiation and then by convection (pp. 26–27), until it reaches the part of the Sun that is visible, the photosphere. Outside the photosphere is the chromosphere, which is something like an atmosphere. It takes thousands of years for energy to travel from the core to the photosphere.

A PROMINENT FEATURE

Often about one-third of the diameter of the Sun, huge eruptions of hot gases like this are called solar prominences. They seem to be linked with sunspots and the Sun's magnetic energy. Sunspots are slightly cooler areas on the surface of the Sun and are seen as darker patches. Prominences often arc between two sunspots. During a solar eclipse, as the Moon passes between the Sun and the Earth, large prominences become visible to the eye.

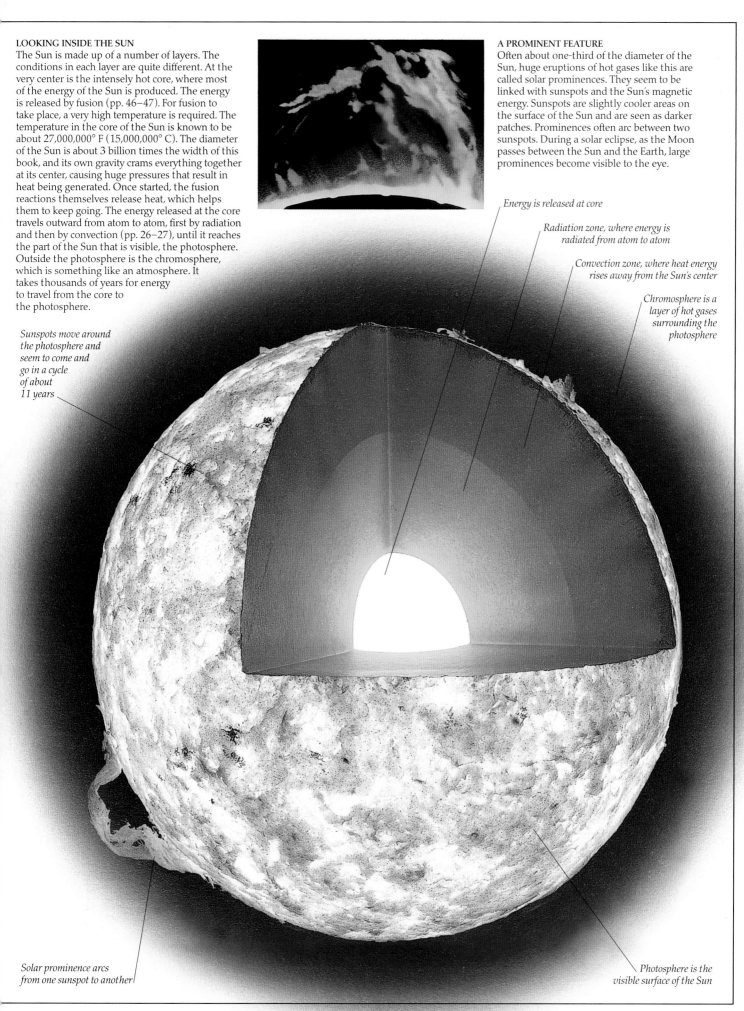

Sunspots move around the photosphere and seem to come and go in a cycle of about 11 years

Solar prominence arcs from one sunspot to another

Energy is released at core

Radiation zone, where energy is radiated from atom to atom

Convection zone, where heat energy rises away from the Sun's center

Chromosphere is a layer of hot gases surrounding the photosphere

Photosphere is the visible surface of the Sun

Photosynthesis

When energy from the Sun (pp. 48–49) falls on plant leaves, it can be stored as chemical potential energy (pp. 14–15) in plants. This is photosynthesis—the process by which light energy is taken into plant cells and stored as it separates oxygen from water. The discovery of photosynthesis was gradual. Toward the end of the 18th century Joseph Priestley (1733–1804), an English chemist, studied the gases involved in burning. He discovered that plants change the quality of the air around them. They do this by taking in what is now known as carbon dioxide and giving out what is now known as oxygen. In 1779, the Dutch scientist Jan Ingenhousz (1730–99) discovered that this happens only when a plant is exposed to light. By the end of the 19th century photosynthesis was understood in terms of energy. It is a process vitally important to life on Earth. Without photosynthesis, there would be no food (pp. 52–53) for humans or other animals. Photosynthesis in plants living millions of years ago converted solar energy into the chemical energy available when fossil fuels (pp. 54–55) are burned.

MAKING SUGAR

In 1864 a German chemist named Julius Sachs (1832–97) discovered which chemicals are involved in photosynthesis. He found that carbon dioxide taken in by plants is combined with hydrogen from water, which is made of oxygen and hydrogen. The energy for this reaction comes from light falling on the plant. The hydrogen and carbon dioxide join to form glucose, a type of sugar that is the food for the plant. Some of the glucose is made into starch, which is a good energy store. The oxygen that is separated from the water is released by the plant.

Carbon dioxide in the jar is gradually replaced by oxygen

Plant cells in the leaves take in carbon dioxide and give out oxygen

Water stops the gases from escaping

Gas jar filled with carbon dioxide

Candle will not burn in the carbon dioxide

PRIESTLEY'S EXPERIMENT

In the 1770s Joseph Priestley was investigating gases. At that time it was believed that burning involved the release of a substance named "phlogiston." When a candle burned, for example, it was thought to be releasing "phlogisticated air." This was a gas that did not allow anything to burn in it and was poisonous to animals. Priestley was surprised to discover that if a plant was placed in the gas, it could "de-phlogisticate" the air, making it breathable again. Priestley discovered the two gases that are now known as carbon dioxide and oxygen.

1 PHLOGISTICATED AIR

Burning will not occur in carbon dioxide gas, and the gas can be deadly if breathed. Priestley obtained samples of the gas (he called it "phlogisticated" air) by burning a small candle in a jar and by collecting the gas as a by-product from the brewery next to his home. It is now known that carbon dioxide is also released as a result of respiration (pp. 52–53), the reverse of photosynthesis.

Water trough

2 PHOTOSYNTHESIS IN ACTION

Priestley left plants in jars full of carbon dioxide. Although he did not know it, the plants were photosynthesizing and taking in the carbon dioxide they needed to make the chemicals necessary to survive and grow. During photosynthesis the plants gave out oxygen gas, which then filled the jars. Priestley experimented with the gas and realized that it had very different properties from the carbon dioxide gas.

Small candle used to fill a jar with carbon dioxide, and to test the gas in a jar

WHAT HAPPENS INSIDE A PLANT CELL

All the complex chemical reactions involved in photosynthesis take place inside the cells of plants in parts of the cell called chloroplasts. Chloroplasts contain a chemical compound called chlorophyll, which absorbs energy from light. In a split second, the energy passes quickly through the chloroplast as tiny currents of electricity, separating atoms of oxygen from water molecules and joining together the hydrogen and the carbon dioxide to form glucose. The glucose is then transported around the plant to wherever it is needed by a network of tubes called the phloem.

Ivy leaves

Green leaves contain a large proportion of chlorophyll

Pink leaves contain a mixture of pigments, including xanthophyll and B-carotene

Chloroplasts in green plants contain chlorophyll

Nucleus controls the activities of the cell

Endoplasmic reticulum transports nutrients within the cell

Green plant leaf

Vacuole stores sap

Cell wall

Coleus leaves

GREEN LEAVES AND PINK LEAVES

Inside the chloroplasts in plant cells there are special chemicals that absorb the light falling on the plant. These chemicals absorb only particular colors of light, reflecting all other colors. The most common of these chemicals is chlorophyll, which reflects green light, giving most plants a green color. However, the mixture of chemicals inside chloroplasts can vary, and some plants have differently colored leaves as a result. These other chemicals work in the same way as chlorophyll. During the fall, the chlorophyll in the leaves of green leafy trees is broken down, revealing the colors of the other chemicals present in the leaves.

3 BURNING PLANT GAS *(below)*

Priestley found that candles burn very well in the gas produced by the plants. Of course, oxygen is used up in burning, so the candles would eventually be extinguished once again. However, if a plant was placed in the jar once this had happened, it would replace the carbon dioxide with oxygen. In photosynthesis, energy is taken in by the plant and oxygen is released. In burning, oxygen is used up and energy is released.

Oxygen is combined with carbon, present in the wax, to produce carbon dioxide

Candle burns well in the oxygen, releasing energy as heat and light

Mouse breathes in the oxygen that was produced by the green plant

4 BREATHING PLANT GAS

Priestley also found that the gas produced by the plants was breathable. When he placed an animal, such as a mouse, in a bell jar that contained oxygen, it was able to breathe normally. Like humans, animals need to breathe oxygen to burn food within the body to obtain energy.

REACHING FOR THE LIGHT

Light is vital to all plants, so plants need to be exposed to as much of it as possible. This is why plants bend toward light. There is a huge variety of plants that photosynthesize. Each has developed its own way of guaranteeing a share of the incoming sunlight. For example, the giant redwood trees of North America can grow to a height of more than 350 ft (100 m). Other plants have evolved to grow in desert or tundra conditions, using the light energy available in places where most other plants would not survive.

Energy from food

SPINACH FOR ENERGY
Popeye, a cartoon character created in the 1930s, becomes incredibly strong when he eats spinach. He was originally intended to promote healthy eating to children. Spinach contains not only energy but also vitamins and minerals, which are other essential parts of food.

ALL LIVING THINGS need energy for a variety of activities, such as growing, moving, and keeping warm. Some, such as plants, capture energy—usually from sunlight—and store it as chemical potential energy (pp. 14–15). Other living things that cannot capture energy in this way have to make use of the energy stored elsewhere. They get this energy by feeding on other animals or plants. Humans eat plants and animals to obtain the energy they need. The food that humans eat is burned, or oxidized, inside the body during digestion. In a similar way, fossil fuels, such as coal and oil, are oxidized when they are ignited. Oxygen from the air combines with a substance that is burned. When fossil fuels burn, they release heat and light in flames. When food is burned in the body, chemical energy is released. Different types of food store and release different amounts of energy. Fat, for example, is a more concentrated energy store than sugar.

FEEDING THEMSELVES
All organisms that make their own food—like these phytoplankton—are called autotrophic, meaning self-feeding. Most autotrophic organisms are plants, which take energy from sunlight by photosynthesis (pp. 50–51).

Food energy values

When food is burned in an animal's body, the chemical potential energy stored within it is released. Different foods release different amounts of energy. The amount of energy released by foods is usually measured in kilocalories (kcal) or joules (J, pp. 36–37)—1 kcal is equal to about 4,200 J, and is also called a calorie. There are three groups of energy-giving chemicals in food—carbohydrates, fats, and proteins.

ENERGY FROM FRUIT
Fruit, such as these grapes, contains natural sugars that provide energy. Each grape provides about 1 kcal. If more sugar is eaten than the body needs, the sugar is converted into fat, a good store of food energy, so that it can be used another time.

ENERGY FROM SUGAR
In the middle of the 19th century, French physiologist Claude Bernard discovered how large carbohydrate molecules are converted to smaller molecules of glucose in the liver. Food containing carbohydrates must first be broken down into glucose, a type of sugar, before its energy can be obtained. The glucose is carried from the liver around the bloodstream and combined with oxygen, releasing energy in a process called "aerobic respiration". In this process, glucose and oxygen become water and carbon dioxide. This is the reverse of photosynthesis (pp. 50–51), in which glucose is made from water and carbon dioxide, and energy is taken in by a plant.

ENERGY FROM POTATOES
This potato contains a lot of starch, which stores the energy that a new plant needs to begin growing. Starch molecules must be broken down in the body into simple sugar molecules before their energy can be released.

Grapes contain 17 calories per oz (28 g)

Potatoes contain about 25 calories per oz (28 g)

Grain contains about 84 calories per oz (28 g)

ENERGY FROM SEEDS
Seeds such as these sunflower seeds contain most of their energy in fats. Many seeds can be eaten whole, and many types are also crushed to release fats in the form of oils, which can be used in cooking.

Sunflower seeds contain about 92 calories per oz (28 g)

ENERGY FROM MEAT
Meat is a good source of energy, and much of its energy is stored in fat. But meat is not a very efficient energy source. For example, only a small amount of the energy taken in by a living chicken can be obtained by someone who eats it.

Roast chicken contains about 84 calories per oz (28 g)

ENERGY FROM GRAIN
Grain is a good source of energy because it is a direct store of the energy of photosynthesis. This type of wheat is grown to be fed to animals, such as cattle. Other types are often ground into flour for human consumption in products such as bread.

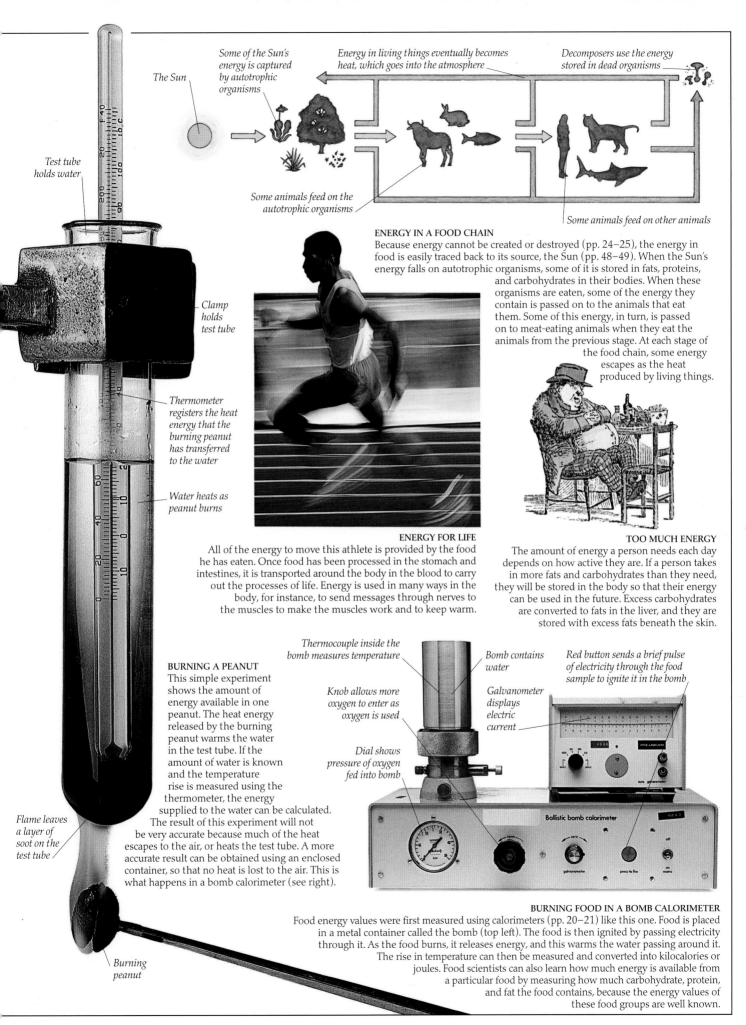

Test tube holds water

Clamp holds test tube

Thermometer registers the heat energy that the burning peanut has transferred to the water

Water heats as peanut burns

Flame leaves a layer of soot on the test tube

Burning peanut

The Sun

Some of the Sun's energy is captured by autotrophic organisms

Energy in living things eventually becomes heat, which goes into the atmosphere

Decomposers use the energy stored in dead organisms

Some animals feed on the autotrophic organisms

Some animals feed on other animals

ENERGY IN A FOOD CHAIN

Because energy cannot be created or destroyed (pp. 24–25), the energy in food is easily traced back to its source, the Sun (pp. 48–49). When the Sun's energy falls on autotrophic organisms, some of it is stored in fats, proteins, and carbohydrates in their bodies. When these organisms are eaten, some of the energy they contain is passed on to the animals that eat them. Some of this energy, in turn, is passed on to meat-eating animals when they eat the animals from the previous stage. At each stage of the food chain, some energy escapes as the heat produced by living things.

ENERGY FOR LIFE

All of the energy to move this athlete is provided by the food he has eaten. Once food has been processed in the stomach and intestines, it is transported around the body in the blood to carry out the processes of life. Energy is used in many ways in the body, for instance, to send messages through nerves to the muscles to make the muscles work and to keep warm.

TOO MUCH ENERGY

The amount of energy a person needs each day depends on how active they are. If a person takes in more fats and carbohydrates than they need, they will be stored in the body so that their energy can be used in the future. Excess carbohydrates are converted to fats in the liver, and they are stored with excess fats beneath the skin.

BURNING A PEANUT

This simple experiment shows the amount of energy available in one peanut. The heat energy released by the burning peanut warms the water in the test tube. If the amount of water is known and the temperature rise is measured using the thermometer, the energy supplied to the water can be calculated. The result of this experiment will not be very accurate because much of the heat escapes to the air, or heats the test tube. A more accurate result can be obtained using an enclosed container, so that no heat is lost to the air. This is what happens in a bomb calorimeter (see right).

Thermocouple inside the bomb measures temperature

Bomb contains water

Red button sends a brief pulse of electricity through the food sample to ignite it in the bomb

Knob allows more oxygen to enter as oxygen is used

Galvanometer displays electric current

Dial shows pressure of oxygen fed into bomb

Ballistic bomb calorimeter

BURNING FOOD IN A BOMB CALORIMETER

Food energy values were first measured using calorimeters (pp. 20–21) like this one. Food is placed in a metal container called the bomb (top left). The food is then ignited by passing electricity through it. As the food burns, it releases energy, and this warms the water passing around it. The rise in temperature can then be measured and converted into kilocalories or joules. Food scientists can also learn how much energy is available from a particular food by measuring how much carbohydrate, protein, and fat the food contains, because the energy values of these food groups are well known.

Fossil fuels

Coal, oil, and natural gas are called fossil fuels. They were formed by the action of bacteria and the pressure of the Earth on the remains of tiny organisms that lived millions of years ago. The energy originally came from the Sun and was stored as chemical potential energy (pp. 14–15) by photosynthesis (pp. 50–51). Coal was the first fossil fuel to be used on a large scale. Raw coal can be burned to provide heat. When coal is heated in a closed vessel without burning, it produces a gas that can be used as fuel. This "coal gas" gave a convenient supply of energy to homes during the 19th century and part of the 20th. "Natural gas" is similar to coal gas. It is often found near oil, which is the fossil fuel that dominated the 20th century. From oil come gasoline and other fuels, which can be burned to release their fossil energy. Humans have released billions of tons of carbon dioxide into the atmosphere by burning fossil fuels. Carbon dioxide is a "greenhouse gas," and scientists have found evidence that increasing the amount of the gas in the atmosphere is causing global warming (pp. 56–57). Thus, it is important to use fossil fuels efficiently.

COLLECTING OIL
In some places oil seeps from rocks called "oil shale." This type of oil is "crude oil," and it has been collected at its source and used for centuries. The oil was once commonly used for lighting, but it was never ideal because when it burns it becomes smelly and smoky.

Steam condenses on the glass vessel

MAKING COAL GAS
Coal is a mixture of many different substances. When it is heated, it breaks down into those substances. In this glass vessel coal is being heated and is releasing coal gas. This gas is being burned at the open end of the vessel. Coal gas is made mainly of hydrogen and methane— the other substances that make up coal remain as solids or thick liquids. Both of these gases burn well, combining with oxygen in the air. As they burn, they release energy that originally came from the Sun. The energy is released as heat and light in the flame. This is why coal gas was used mainly for heating and lighting in streets, homes, and factories.

Lumps of coal are heated, but not burned

Filter prevents the flames from coming into contact with the glass vessel

ANCIENT FOREST
About 300 million years ago much of the Earth was covered with swamps and forests, full of plants. These plants were a natural store of chemical energy from photosynthesis. When the plants died, some of them were buried. Under the right conditions they slowly turned into coal over

Bunsen burner flame provides heat energy

Clamp holds the glass vessel away from the flame so it does not overheat

HOW OIL AND GAS ARE FORMED

Oil has been used on a large scale only since it was first drilled in Pennsylvania in 1859. Natural gas—made mainly of methane—has replaced coal gas because it is more convenient and the same volume releases more energy. Oil and natural gas are usually found together.

1 SUN AND SEA
Like coal, the story of the formation of oil and gas begins millions of years ago when the Sun's energy was stored in tiny marine organisms, such as algae and plankton. Instead of decaying in the usual way when they died, they were buried in layers of sediment, such as sand and salt.

Sea

Millions of tiny marine organisms

Older layers of sediment

Lower layer of rock

2 BACTERIAL ACTION
Over millions of years the chemicals that made up the organisms were converted into oil and natural gas as bacteria and the pressure of more layers of sediment broke them down. The pressure of the moving rocks of the Earth caused the layers to be "folded" or broken. The oil and natural gas often collected in the resulting shapes.

Marine organisms are buried in layers of sediment

New layers are constantly being formed

Layers of rock and sediment are folded by huge pressures as the Earth shifts

3 RISING ENERGY
Oil and natural gas are less dense than water, so they can rise through "permeable" rocks, which are not solid. They then collect underneath an "impermeable," or solid, layer of rock called a caprock. By studying rock formations, the site of oil and natural gas can be predicted with great accuracy.

Natural gas rig

Oil rig

Natural gas site

Oil site

Both fuels collect under caprock

Gas and oil have seeped up through layers of permeable rock

HOW TO FIND THE CALORIFIC VALUE

It is often necessary to find out how much energy is available in fossil fuels. For example, engineers need to know the "energy content"—or calorific value—of a fuel that powers an engine. A calorimeter (pp. 20–21) can be used to discover the calorific value of a given fuel. The gas calorimeter shown here was designed by the British scientist Charles Boys (1855–1944). A steady supply of gas is burned inside, and this heats a steady supply of water. By measuring the temperature rise in the water, the calorific value of the burning gas can be calculated. One cubic meter (34 cubic ft) of coal gas releases about 19 million joules (pp. 36–37). The same volume of natural gas releases about twice as much energy.

Small microscope allows accurate readings to be taken

Thermometer measures the temperature of water leaving calorimeter

Thermometer measures the temperature of water entering calorimeter

Water flows out of this tap

Water flows in through this tap

Gas enters the apparatus through this tap

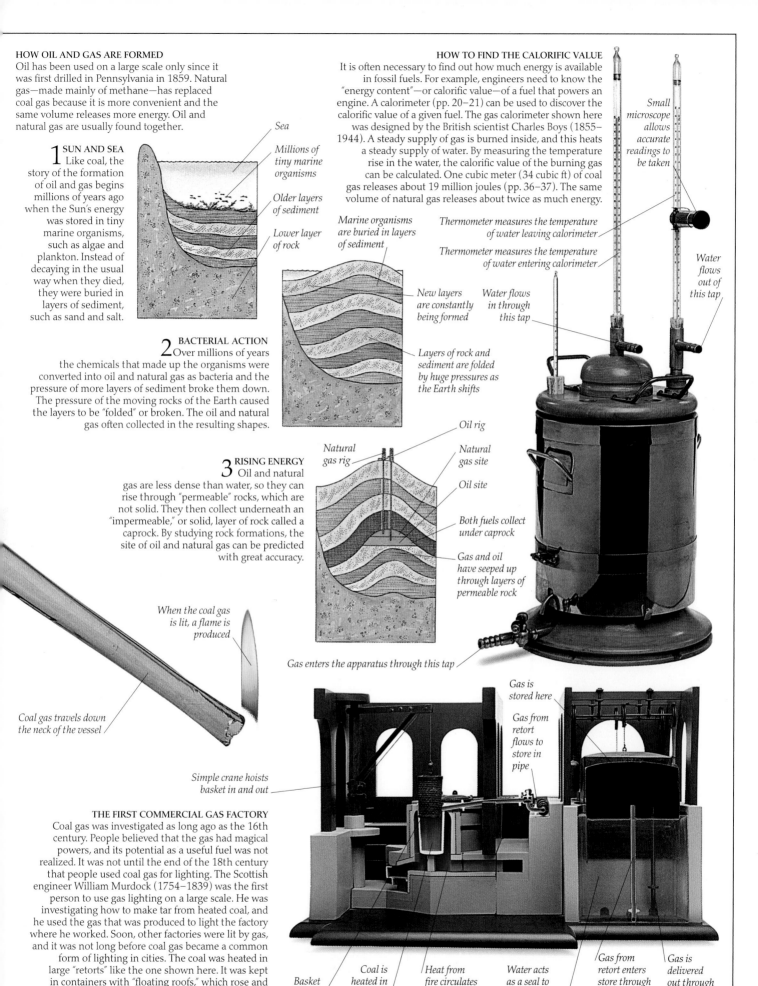

When the coal gas is lit, a flame is produced

Coal gas travels down the neck of the vessel

Gas is stored here

Gas from retort flows to store in pipe

Simple crane hoists basket in and out

THE FIRST COMMERCIAL GAS FACTORY

Coal gas was investigated as long ago as the 16th century. People believed that the gas had magical powers, and its potential as a useful fuel was not realized. It was not until the end of the 18th century that people used coal gas for lighting. The Scottish engineer William Murdock (1754–1839) was the first person to use gas lighting on a large scale. He was investigating how to make tar from heated coal, and he used the gas that was produced to light the factory where he worked. Soon, other factories were lit by gas, and it was not long before coal gas became a common form of lighting in cities. The coal was heated in large "retorts" like the one shown here. It was kept in containers with "floating roofs," which rose and fell as the amount of gas in the container changed.

Basket holds coal

Coal is heated in retorts

Heat from fire circulates around the retort

Water acts as a seal to keep the gas in

Gas from retort enters store through this pipe

Gas is delivered out through this pipe

Energy on a global scale

MOST OF THE ENERGY WE USE TODAY for heating, for transportation (pp. 30–31), and for generating electricity (pp. 32–33) comes from burning fossil fuels (pp. 54–55). But at the rate we are using them, oil and gas may run out within a few decades, and coal within 200 years. There is another problem with our insatiable demand for fossil fuels. When they are burned, fossil fuels release carbon dioxide into the atmosphere. Carbon dioxide is a "greenhouse gas"—it warms the planet's surface by absorbing heat energy that would otherwise escape into space. In the last 100 years, there has been a steady rise in our planet's average temperature, which climate scientists put down to the huge amount of carbon dioxide released by burning fossil fuels. To make supplies of fossil fuels last longer, and to reduce the threat of global warming, it is important to search for alternative sources of energy (pp. 58–59) that are "carbon neutral," and to reduce our demand for energy (pp. 60–61).

TERMITES AND METHANE
Many animals, such as termites, make methane, a strong greenhouse gas, in their digestive systems. Although termites are small, there are so many of them that the methane they produce affects the quality of the air on a global scale. In a similar way, the humans are adding extra carbon dioxide to the atmosphere.

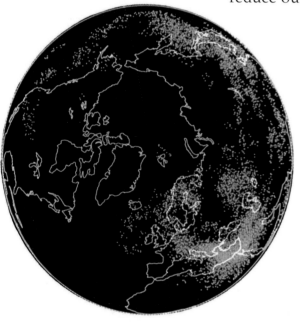

NUCLEAR DISASTER
About 13 percent of the world's electricity is generated in nuclear power plants (pp. 46–47). Radioactive waste has to be buried underground—a potential problem for future generations. Sometimes, serious accidents at nuclear power plants release radioactive substances into the environment. The pink areas on the map above show parts of the world that received radioactive contamination after the worst-ever nuclear accident on April 26, 1986, at Chernobyl, Ukraine.

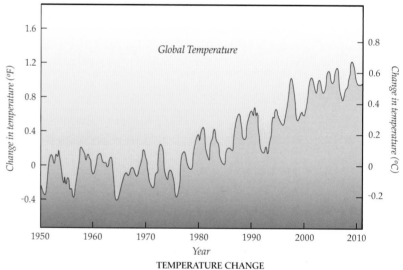

Global Temperature

(chart: Change in temperature (°F) vs Year, 1950–2010; secondary axis Change in temperature (°C))

TEMPERATURE CHANGE
Earth's average surface temperature has risen by 1.6° F (0.9° C) over the last 100 years. The temperature rise is speeding up—1.0° F (0.6° C) of the increase has happened since 1960. By looking at other signs of temperature, such as the thickness of tree rings, scientists have extended the record of temperature back thousands of years, for comparison. Most scientists agree that the recent global warming is mostly due to the billions of tons of carbon dioxide released by the burning of fossil fuels. Carbon dioxide is one of the "greenhouse gases" that absorbs heat energy that would otherwise be lost to space.

SEA OF CONCERN
If emissions of carbon dioxide continue—and if the global temperature continues to increase as a result—then the polar ice caps will continue to melt, causing the world's sea levels to rise. Droughts and floods will become more common, crop yields will suffer, and many plant and animal species will become extinct.

Sun's energy comes to the Earth at a nearly constant rate

The US uses about one-third of the total available energy but has only one-twentieth of the population

Some Scandinavian countries obtain much of their energy from hydroelectric power

Most of the fossil fuels used by the world's population is obtained from the Middle East

Energy used per person in Gigajoules (billions of Joules, GJ)
- 0–60
- 61–130
- 130–190
- 190–260
- >260

Each person in India uses an average of about 3 GJ each year

ENERGY USED BY PEOPLE
This map shows the differences in energy use between the developed and the less-developed countries of the world. In developed countries, energy is obtained mainly from fossil fuels. In many less-developed countries, people still depend on muscle energy for their needs. Since people in developed countries have more vehicles and electrical appliances, they use more energy than people living in the less-developed countries.

THE LIVING EARTH
In 1979 the British scientist James Lovelock put forward the idea that the Earth and all life on it is one huge living organism. He named the organism Gaia, after the Greek Earth goddess. This picture shows Lovelock with a statue of the goddess Gaia. He suggested that Gaia is responsible for keeping the conditions in the sea and on the land right for Gaia to carry on living. Now that the population of Earth and its energy use have grown so large, humans can affect land, sea, and air in ways that throw Gaia off balance.

Amount of energy in reserve is falling as energy use increases

Humans can control their energy use

Earth's store of energy is mostly fossil fuels

IN-FLOW AND OUT-FLOW
Imagine the Earth as a container, into which flows the energy from the Sun (pp. 48–49), and out of which flows the energy used by human beings, which ends up as useless heat energy. When fossil fuels were formed, the container was full. For the past few hundred years, humans have used the energy from fossil fuels at an incredible rate. The faucet at the bottom of the container is being opened more and more. One day the store of energy from fossil fuels will run out. Only by closing the faucet a little, and by making more use of the Sun's energy flowing in, will the human race avoid a worldwide energy crisis.

Humans use energy at a rate of about 1,000 million million million J each year

Alternative energy

IF THE HUMAN RACE CONTINUES to use fossil fuels on as large a scale as the present (pp. 56–57), then reserves of oil, coal, and natural gas will begin to dwindle and global warming may threaten our way of life (pp. 56–57). One solution is to use fossil fuels more efficiently (pp. 60–61) by being less wasteful. There are other sources of energy that can be used for heating, transportation, and to generate electricity. These sources will not run out—they are renewable and do not release carbon dioxide. Examples of these alternative energy sources include solar power, which can be used even by countries that are not hot (pp. 48–49)—wind power, hydroelectric power, and wave power.

Prototype of an energy-harvesting device known as a Salter Duck

Beak of duck nods up and down with the wave

Behind the duck, water is calm, because the energy of the wave has been absorbed

SOLAR PRINTING PRESS
There have been many ingenious inventions to provide a supply of energy in case of a shortage of fossil fuels. The French engineer Abel Pifre invented this solar printing press, which he demonstrated in Paris in 1882. Sunlight that shone into its 10½ ft (3.5 m) diameter concave mirror was focused on to a steam boiler to heat the water inside. The steam that was produced then powered an engine that in turn provided the energy for the printing press. On the day of Pifre's demonstration, his press printed more than 2,000 copies of a special publication that he called the *Soleil-Journal*, or *Sun Journal*.

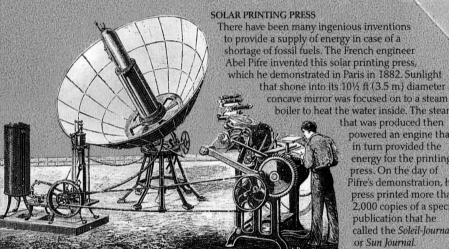

Nozzle through which jet of water flows

Pairs of buckets stop the water, taking most of its kinetic energy

Pelton wheel, also known as the jet-splitting double-bucket turbine (below and right)

Water-pressure gauge

Cutaway section shows buckets

Flywheel

Water enters here

Belt driven by Pelton wheel connects to generator

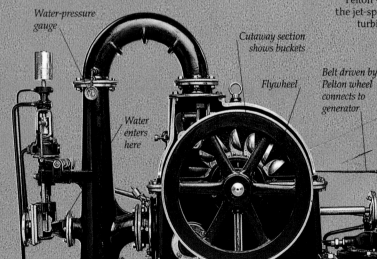

HYDROELECTRIC ENERGY
Water turbines like this Pelton wheel are used to produce electricity in hydroelectric power plants. Hydroelectric power is created when the potential energy (pp. 14–15) of water held in a reservoir above a turbine is changed to kinetic energy as the water is released through a nozzle. The water turns a turbine, which is connected to a generator. The rate at which electrical energy is produced depends on how fast the water flows and how far above the turbine the reservoir is. The Pelton wheel was designed by the American mining engineer Lester Pelton (1829–1908).

ENERGY FROM THE SEA

The object on the opposite page is a prototype of an energy-harvesting device known as a Salter Duck (see opposite). Designed in the 1970s by British engineer Stephen Salter, the duck was the first practical device to extract energy from waves. It bobs up and down, absorbing the waves' energy. The movement of the duck pushes liquid through tubes, and the liquid turns a generator to produce electricity. Today, there are many other similar wave power devices and some large-scale trials. As another alternative, turbines placed in tidal water can extract energy from the force of its flow and generate electricity from it.

CHARGING UP THE BATTERIES

Electric vehicles produce no carbon dioxide or other pollutants and are quieter than conventional gas- or diesel-powered vehicles. If the batteries are recharged using electricity generated using alternative, renewable sources, then no carbon dioxide is generated in the energy supply chain either. The first electric cars were built in the 1890s, but gas and diesel vehicles were much more popular while fossil fuels were cheap and plentiful. With concerns about global warming and worries about the availability of crude oil, electric cars may be much more popular in the future.

Crest of wave

Water moves up and down as wave passes but does not move along with the wave

BIOMASS

These wood chips are about to be broken down chemically to produce methane gas. This gas can be burned to produce heat and electricity. Wood is an example of "biomass"—energy-rich material from plants. Sugar cane, corn, and even agricultural waste can be used as biomass, too. As with fossil fuels, biomass releases carbon dioxide when it burns. But burning biomass is "carbon neutral"—a plant absorbed the same amount of carbon dioxide in its recent lifetime as it produced when burned. It is reneweable, too, as new plants can be grown to replace those used as biomass.

WIND POWER

People have been harnessing the kinetic energy of wind for centuries (pp. 12–13), but wind power was not used to generate electricity until the 1880s. With the need to reduce our use of fossil fuels, wind turbines have become ever more commonplace in the landscape—and out at sea. Turbines can be small— providing energy for a small motor home or cabin, for example— or huge structures that provide energy for many homes. In particularly windy locations, many wind turbines may be built together, forming a wind farm (above).

ENERGY FROM HOT ROCKS

This power plant in Iceland uses geothermal energy, which is heat energy from beneath the surface of the Earth, to produce hot water and steam. The steam drives turbines that generate nearly 3,000,000 J of electrical energy per second, and the hot water is piped to homes. Much of the heat energy comes from molten rocks underground.

Making the most of energy

During the past 100 years, the world's demand for energy has grown enormously (pp. 56–57). Most of the demand has been met by burning fossil fuels (pp. 54–55). But fossil fuel is a nonrenewable energy source, and reserves may begin to dwindle in the next few decades. Also, the carbon dioxide released by burning fossil fuels is thought to lead to global warming. It is important to use alternatives to fossil fuels (pp. 58–59), but alternative sources alone cannot satisfy our increasing demand. So, it is also important to use less energy and to make the best of the energy we do use. There are many ways to do this. For example, public transportation tends to be more efficient than cars, because the fuel is shared among more people. When we recycle and reuse things, we use much less energy than when we make new things. This helps in reducing the amount of energy we use. Traveling less, insulating buildings, and simply switching off lights and appliances, are other important ways to make the most of energy.

MAKING THE MOST OF A ROCKING CHAIR
One way to make the most of energy is to use energy that would otherwise be wasted. This "New Domestic Motor," invented (by a man!) in 1873, made use of "the latent feminine energy." It allowed three jobs to be done at once. As the worker rocked in the rocking chair, sewing or doing other handiwork, a system of levers, weights, and pulleys was set in motion. This rocked a baby and churned butter at the same time.

SAME LIGHT, LESS ENERGY
For most of the 20th century, most electric lighting used incandescent lamps—glass bulbs containing a fine metal filament, which glowed because it was hot. Nearly all the energy supplied to an incandescent lamp ends up as heat energy (pp. 20–21) in the filament, and is lost. Modern compact fluorescent bulbs are increasingly replacing incandescent ones, because they are about four times as efficient at converting electrical energy into light. In the demonstration below, the two lamps are producing about the same amount of light, but the incandescent lamp uses much more electrical energy.

Bulbs produce the same amount of light

60-watt bulb

18-watt bulb

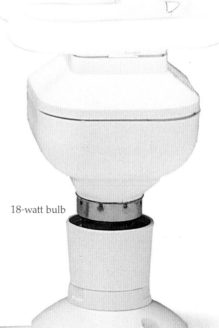

Incandescent bulb uses over twice the electricity per second as the fluorescent bulb

Fluorescent bulb uses much less energy per second than the incandescent bulb

Cable carries electricity

THE SUN CAN HELP

In most countries the Sun is not reliable or powerful enough to provide all the energy a household needs. However, the Sun's energy can be used to supplement other energy sources. Solar collectors like this one, installed on the roof, can use the Sun's energy to heat water for household use. If the Sun is not intense enough on a particular day, then a gas or electric boiler is used, but on sunnier days the solar collector can supply the needs of a household. The electricity or gas is used only when necessary, and so less energy is wasted.

Pipes hold water for heating

Steel wool insulates the water pipes

Two layers of metal foil reflect radiant energy back on to water pipes

Light aluminum frame

Transparent film allows radiation from the Sun to be converted into energy

INSULATING THE HOME

Most homes do not use energy efficiently. Heat is lost through windows, walls, and the roof. This means that more energy is needed to keep the house warm. There are many things that can be done to a house to improve its energy efficiency, such as installing double-paned windows, draft proofing, and insulating ceilings, walls, floors, and hot-water heaters. Insulating the attic keeps the house warm in the winter and cool in the summer. Most modern homes are insulated while they are being built, but it is also possible to add insulation to an older home.

SECOND TIME AROUND

This pile of used plastic is waiting to be recycled, rather than being thrown away. To recycle this plastic, it must be heated so that it melts and can be molded into a new shape. Glass (pp. 10–11) can be recycled in a similar way. Recycling is an important way of making the most of energy, because less energy is needed to make things out of recycled materials than if manufacturers start with raw materials. Many people throw things away when they are no longer needed, but this is a waste of the energy that was put into making them, and can cause pollution. Buying fewer unnecessary goods and reusing items are other important ways to be energy efficient.

NEWSPAPER LOGS

Using things again, whether for the same purpose or for something else, can help reduce energy waste. A good deal of energy can be obtained from many materials by burning them. Some countries burn much of their garbage in power plants and use the heat that is released to make steam that powers electricity generators. A similar thing can be done on a smaller scale. These logs are made from old newspapers, which are often thrown away after they have been read. Logs like these burn for up to two hours, providing a cheap way to heat a home. Another way paper can be used again is to make it into recycled paper.

Newspapers are soaked in water and placed into this machine to compress them

Compressed and dried newspaper logs

The origins and destiny of energy

THE UNIVERSE IS TRULY VAST. The Earth is part of the solar system, centered around the Sun. The Sun is one tiny part of a collection of 100 billion stars in a galaxy called the Milky Way. This is just one of a huge group of galaxies. There are millions upon millions of other galaxies, separated by enormous distances of almost empty space. In that space is the light and other radiation given off by countless stars like the Sun (pp. 48–49). All of the radiation and all of the matter that make up the universe are forms of energy. At the centers of stars, matter is constantly being lost, but an equivalent amount of energy is always released as a result.

Energy condenses into matter

AN OPEN AND SHUT UNIVERSE
According to Hindu myths, many universes are created by the god Vishnu when he opens and shuts his eyes. As he opens his eyes, he dreams, and his dream is a new universe. After many millions of years, he shuts his eyes and that universe ends. Some scientists believe that the universe may one day collapse on itself, to be reborn in a new Big Bang. This could repeat for ever, with a different universe resulting each time, just as each of Vishnu's dreams would have been different.

The universe is not infinitely large, but it seems to have begun with a "Big Bang," in which a fixed amount of energy came from nothing. Some scientists say that this fixed amount of energy is available for only a fixed amount of time, and that one day the universe will be squashed out of existence in a "Big Crunch".

THE BIG BANG
Observations of the stars and galaxies that make up the universe suggest that they are all moving apart. This means that the very space of which the universe is made is expanding—stretching like the rubber skin of a huge balloon. If this is true then at some time, about 13.7 billion years ago, all of space and time must have come out of nothing, possibly in a huge explosion now called the Big Bang.

1 SINGLE POINT OF ENERGY
According to the Big Bang theory, all space and time were created at a single point far smaller than an atom. That point must have contained all the energy of the universe, and because all of space was so small, it must have been incredibly hot. At such high temperatures the forces we know today, such as gravity, would have been very different. There would have been no matter—only heat energy would have existed.

2 A SUDDEN INFLATION OF SPACE
Just after the moment of creation, space and time itself began to expand at an incredible rate. This was not an explosion in space, but an inflation of space. It is thought that the reason for the inflation was that, at such high energies, gravity may become a push rather than a pull force.

3 FORMING MATTER
At the end of the very rapid inflation, the universe became cooler, and the particles that make up matter began to form out of some of the energy. Just as water vapor condenses to form water droplets as it cools, so matter was formed from "condensed" energy as the universe cooled.

Robert Wilson (left) and Arno Penzias after winning the 1978 Nobel Prize for their discovery

ECHOES OF THE BIG BANG
In 1964 two American physicists, Robert Wilson and Arno Penzias, detected electromagnetic radiation (pp. 40–41), which exactly fit the predictions of the Big Bang theory. The total amount of energy in the universe is fixed, and it cannot be destroyed. Much of the energy took the form of matter in the early universe, but some of it still remains as a "record" of the Big Bang. This record is the radiation that Wilson and Penzias detected.

EXPLORING THE RIPPLES
In 1992 the American COBE (Cosmic Background Explorer) satellite gathered information about the radiation that fills space. When information from the whole sky was put together and enhanced by a computer, it showed that the universe is not quite the same in every direction. The patches on the picture show that space in the early universe was not even but contained irregular "ripples," around which energy in the form of matter gathered. This seems to explain why matter is lumped together in some places and not in others.

The universe continues
to expand

The universe appears to be flat
but may actually be curved

Between galaxies is
mostly empty space

Galaxies form from
condensing matter

4 A LUMPY UNIVERSE
If the universe were perfectly
smooth as it expanded, it would not
be "lumpy" as it is observed to be. The
young universe was very slightly irregular,
and gravity pulled together the newly formed
matter into galaxies, which give space its "lumpiness."

5 CURVED SPACE AND THE END OF TIME
According to the theory of the Big Bang, the universe
continues to expand, and this fits with the observation that galaxies
are moving apart. If this theory is correct, space should be "curved" like
the surface of an inflating balloon. From the Earth, space seems to be "flat,"
but it could be very slightly curved, hardly noticeable to us because of the expansion.

The energy industry

FOR THE PAST FEW HUNDRED YEARS, people in developed countries have had access to large and ever-increasing amounts of power, for lighting, cooking, transportation, and for industrial purposes. Most of that power has come from burning fossil fuels (pp. 54–55). However, in recent decades, supplies from nuclear power (pp. 46–47) and alternative energy sources have increased. This is partly a result of worries over reserves of fossil fuels running low and partly a result of concerns over the amount of carbon dioxide released into the atmosphere when they are burned.

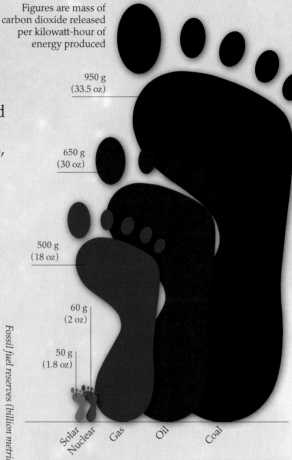

Figures are mass of carbon dioxide released per kilowatt-hour of energy produced

950 g (33.5 oz)

650 g (30 oz)

500 g (18 oz)

60 g (2 oz)

50 g (1.8 oz)

Solar · Nuclear · Gas · Oil · Coal

CARBON FOOTPRINT
The amount of carbon dioxide released by a certain activity is that activity's carbon footprint. The burning of fossil fuels releases large amounts of the gas directly. However, even producing energy from alternative sources (pp. 58–59), such as solar power, leaves a footprint. For example, fuels are burned during the manufacture, maintenance, and transportation of solar panels.

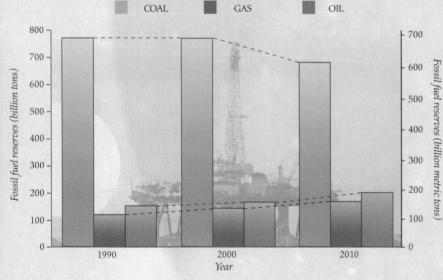

COAL   GAS   OIL

Fossil fuel reserves (billion tons) — 800, 700, 600, 500, 400, 300, 200, 100, 0

Fossil fuel reserves (billion metric tons) — 700, 600, 500, 400, 300, 200, 100, 0

Year — 1990, 2000, 2010

FOSSIL FUEL RESERVES
The chart above shows the "proved reserves"—the amount of each fuel that can be recovered economically (at a profit). Rising prices have made more oil and gas deposits economical—so those graphs rise steadily. Coal prices fell in 2009, making some of the known deposits uneconomical—which is why the coal graph dips in 2010. However, reserves of coal will still outlive reserves of oil and gas. At the present rate of production and use, there is enough coal to last for more than 100 years; oil and natural gas may last for only about 50 years.

GLOBAL ENERGY OUTPUT
As a result of rapid population growth and widening access to energy, the amount of energy used by the world's population has risen steeply over the last few decades. Fossil fuels continue to dominate the supply, but nuclear and hydroelectric power are now playing a greater role. Other renewable sources (see opposite) account for less than 1 percent of the total, and are not shown here. So that different energy sources can be grouped together, the figures in this chart are given in "millions of tons of oil equivalent" (mtoe).

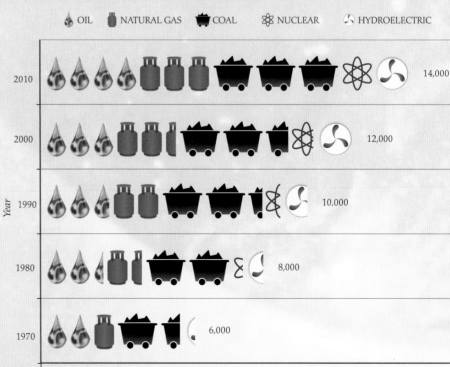

OIL   NATURAL GAS   COAL   NUCLEAR   HYDROELECTRIC

Year		
2010		14,000
2000		12,000
1990		10,000
1980		8,000
1970		6,000

Global uses by energy sources (mtoe)

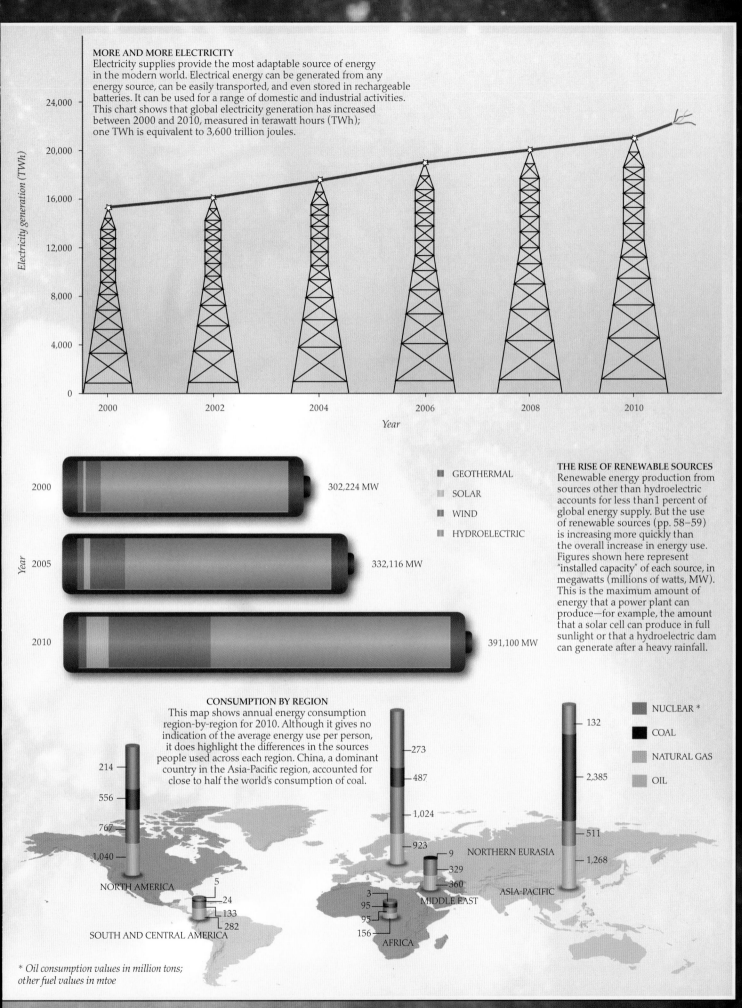

MORE AND MORE ELECTRICITY
Electricity supplies provide the most adaptable source of energy in the modern world. Electrical energy can be generated from any energy source, can be easily transported, and even stored in rechargeable batteries. It can be used for a range of domestic and industrial activities. This chart shows that global electricity generation has increased between 2000 and 2010, measured in terawatt hours (TWh); one TWh is equivalent to 3,600 trillion joules.

Electricity generation (TWh)

24,000
20,000
16,000
12,000
8,000
4,000
0

2000   2002   2004   2006   2008   2010

Year

Year

2000   302,224 MW

2005   332,116 MW

2010   391,100 MW

GEOTHERMAL
SOLAR
WIND
HYDROELECTRIC

THE RISE OF RENEWABLE SOURCES
Renewable energy production from sources other than hydroelectric accounts for less than1 percent of global energy supply. But the use of renewable sources (pp. 58–59) is increasing more quickly than the overall increase in energy use. Figures shown here represent "installed capacity" of each source, in megawatts (millions of watts, MW). This is the maximum amount of energy that a power plant can produce—for example, the amount that a solar cell can produce in full sunlight or that a hydroelectric dam can generate after a heavy rainfall.

CONSUMPTION BY REGION
This map shows annual energy consumption region-by-region for 2010. Although it gives no indication of the average energy use per person, it does highlight the differences in the sources people used across each region. China, a dominant country in the Asia-Pacific region, accounted for close to half the world's consumption of coal.

NUCLEAR *
COAL
NATURAL GAS
OIL

214
556
767
1,040

NORTH AMERICA

5
24
133
282

SOUTH AND CENTRAL AMERICA

273
487
1,024
923

3
95
95
156

AFRICA

9
329
360

MIDDLE EAST

NORTHERN EURASIA

132

2,385

511

1,268

ASIA-PACIFIC

* Oil consumption values in million tons;
other fuel values in mtoe

65

Energy flow

Everything that happens involves energy changing from one form to other forms. For example, an electric light bulb converts electrical energy into light energy, but some of the electrical energy is also lost as heat given out by the bulb. The total amount of energy in any process remains the same. All the energy changes can be tracked and visualized using Sankey diagrams, which are graphic illustrations to show flow, with arrows that are proportional to the magnitude of the flow. The supply of energy for the human body is chemical energy in food. The body stores energy, since the rate at which it needs energy depends on what activity the body is carrying out.

INCANDESCENT BULB IS 5 PERCENT EFFICIENT

5 joules per second of light produced

100 joules per second input of electrical energy

95 joules per second of heat energy

FLUORESCENT ENERGY-SAVING BULB IS 20 PERCENT EFFICIENT

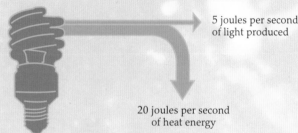

5 joules per second of light produced

25 joules per second input of electrical energy

20 joules per second of heat energy

ELECTRICITY TO LIGHT

In any device or process, only a proportion of the energy input is converted into the desired energy form. There is always some unwanted heat—and often sound—produced, too. The proportion of input energy converted to the desired form or forms of energy is called the efficiency, and is usually expressed as a percentage. The Sankey diagrams above compare two bright bulbs producing the same amount of light energy, but with very different efficiencies.

MOVING A CAR

Scientists and engineers often use Sankey diagrams to visualize the transfers of energy happening in a device or process. The engine inside a typical car produces kinetic (movement) energy (pp. 16–17), but also a lot of heat. Some of the kinetic energy is used to generate electricity and the rest powers the wheels.

Dynamo produces 5,000 joules electricity for headlight, radio, air conditioning, spark plugs

3,000 joules heat lost through friction in gears and transmission

Engine produces 70,000 joules of kinetic energy per second

4,000 joules lost to the air as kinetic energy and heat, through air resistance (drag)

6,000 joules heat lost through friction in the road wheels

Atmosphere

28,000 joules heat energy lost in the exhaust

24,000 joules heat energy lost in the radiator, to cool the engine

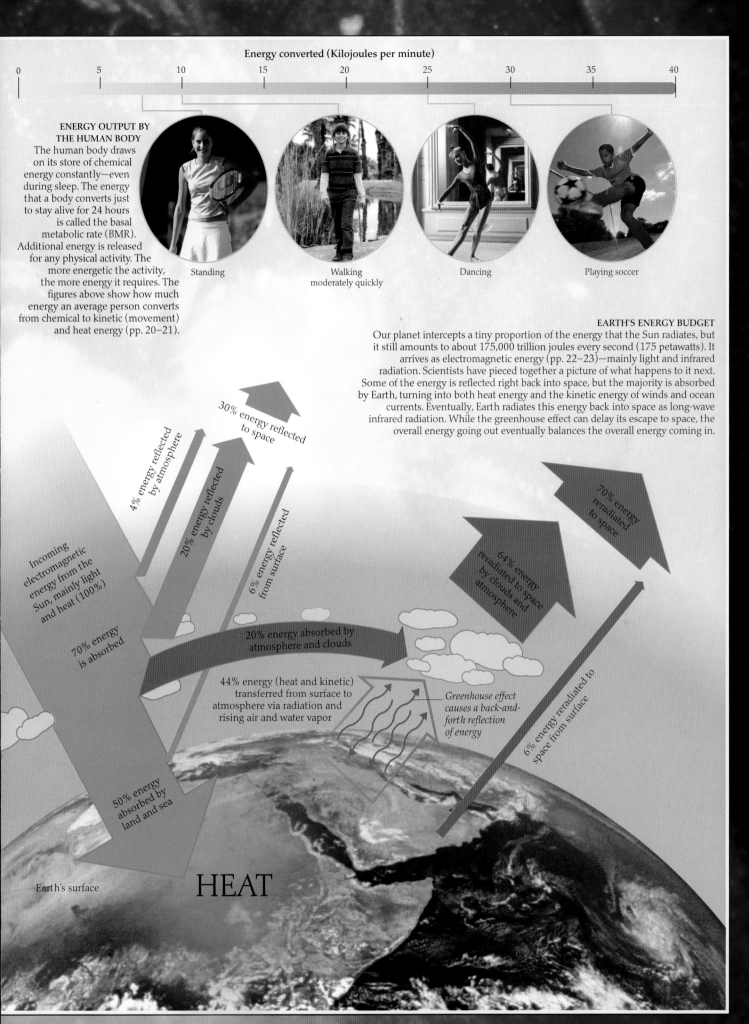

Energy converted (Kilojoules per minute)

0   5   10   15   20   25   30   35   40

ENERGY OUTPUT BY THE HUMAN BODY
The human body draws on its store of chemical energy constantly—even during sleep. The energy that a body converts just to stay alive for 24 hours is called the basal metabolic rate (BMR). Additional energy is released for any physical activity. The more energetic the activity, the more energy it requires. The figures above show how much energy an average person converts from chemical to kinetic (movement) and heat energy (pp. 20–21).

Standing

Walking moderately quickly

Dancing

Playing soccer

EARTH'S ENERGY BUDGET
Our planet intercepts a tiny proportion of the energy that the Sun radiates, but it still amounts to about 175,000 trillion joules every second (175 petawatts). It arrives as electromagnetic energy (pp. 22–23)—mainly light and infrared radiation. Scientists have pieced together a picture of what happens to it next. Some of the energy is reflected right back into space, but the majority is absorbed by Earth, turning into both heat energy and the kinetic energy of winds and ocean currents. Eventually, Earth radiates this energy back into space as long-wave infrared radiation. While the greenhouse effect can delay its escape to space, the overall energy going out eventually balances the overall energy coming in.

30% energy reflected to space

4% energy reflected by atmosphere

20% energy reflected by clouds

6% energy reflected from surface

70% energy reradiated to space

64% energy reradiated to space by clouds and atmosphere

Incoming electromagnetic energy from the Sun, mainly light and heat (100%)

70% energy is absorbed

20% energy absorbed by atmosphere and clouds

44% energy (heat and kinetic) transferred from surface to atmosphere via radiation and rising air and water vapor

Greenhouse effect causes a back-and-forth reflection of energy

6% energy reradiated to space from surface

50% energy absorbed by land and sea

Earth's surface

HEAT

Timeline

Early humans had access only to the energy of their own muscles. When they settled and began farming, they used animal power to help them work the land. The energy of wind, moving water, and fire helped to build civilizations, and these energy sources played a huge role in the Industrial Revolution, which began in Britain in the 18th century. Scientists began to understand energy in the 1840s—and soon after, the development of the internal combustion engine and electric power plants set the modern world on course.

FIRST USE OF FIRE
It is not known exactly when, but around 300,000 years ago, humans begin using the energy of fire to break rocks, cook food, and provide heat and light.

4000 BCE USE OF ANIMAL POWER
People begin using oxen to pull plows. Around the same time, people begin riding horses, and by 3000 BCE, horses and oxen are first used to pull carts.

3000 BCE FIRST SAILING BOATS
Ancient Egyptian boat builders construct the first sails, which use wind energy to help push their boats through the water.

300 BCE FIRST SIMPLE MACHINES
Greek engineer Archimedes develops an understanding of simple machines such as levers, screws, and pulleys, which can make better use of supplied energy and can be incorporated into more complicated machines.

300 BCE FIRST WATER WHEELS
Ancient Greek engineers develop the water wheel and use it in mills to grind grain. Within 100 years, water power is driving bellows and other simple machines.

1ST CENTURY CE WIND POWER
Greek engineer Heron of Alexandria builds an organ played by wind power.

Illustration of the Greek engineer Archimedes, who developed an understanding of simple machines

6TH CENTURY CE FIRST TIDAL MILL
Engineers in Ireland build the first water wheel driven by the movement of water caused by the tides.

9TH CENTURY CE FIRST WINDMILLS
Wind power is first used to grind grain, in Persia (now Iran). Early windmills had sails arranged on a vertical axis.

9TH CENTURY CE GUNPOWDER
Chinese alchemists invent gunpowder, whose rapid release of heat energy revolutionizes warfare and quarrying.

1712 STEAM ENGINE
English engineer Thomas Newcomen designs and builds the first successful steam engine, which pumps water from a flooded mine using the energy released by burning coal.

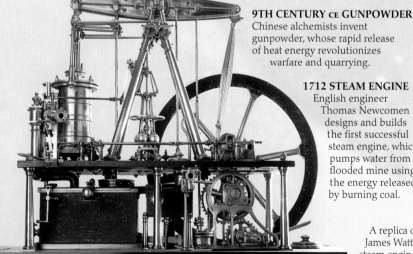

A replica of James Watt's steam engine, 18th century

1765 WATT'S STEAM ENGINE
Scottish engineer James Watt improves the design of steam engines, making them more powerful and more efficient, and therefore able to drive factory machines.

1783 CALORIC
French chemist Antoine Lavoisier coins the term "caloric" for a theoretical weightless substance scientists had suggested might be responsible for heat transfer.

1792 CALORIMETER
Lavoisier invents the calorimeter—a device that measures how quickly substances lose heat, or how much heat a substance generates.

1799 FIRST BATTERY
Italian scientist Alessandro Volta invents the "voltaic pile"—the world's first battery.

1819 ELECTROMAGNETISM
Danish scientist Hans Christian Oersted discovers that an electric current produces a magnetic effect, discovering electromagnetism.

1821 ELECTRIC MOTOR
English scientist Michael Faraday builds a very basic electric motor, which shows how electromagnetism can create continuous motion.

1829 KINETIC ENERGY
French physicist Gustave-Gaspard de Coriolis coins the term "kinetic energy," relating to the energy of moving objects.

1830s OIL INDUSTRY
Engineers in the then Russian Empire extract oil from wells to fuel lamps. The oil industry develops rapidly there, then in North America, and Europe later in the 19th century.

1832 DYNAMO
French physicist Hippolyte Pixii builds the first electric generator. Pixii's device is a dynamo—a generator that produces direct current.

1840s CONSERVATION OF ENERGY
English physicist James Joule shows that heat and "work" are directly related and that energy can neither be created nor destroyed; it only changes form, and so the total amount of energy remains constant.

Hermann von
Helmholtz

1847 CONSERVATION OF ENERGY
German physicist Hermann von Helmholtz publishes the first modern explanation of the fact that energy is never created nor destroyed, only changed from one form to another.

1853 POTENTIAL ENERGY
Scottish physicist William Rankine coins the term "potential energy," relating to stored energy that has the potential to change to a different form.

1855 OIL REFINERY
Polish engineer Ignacy Łukasiewicz builds the first oil refinery to extract useful compounds from crude oil.

1865 ELECTROMAGNETIC RADIATION
Scottish mathematician James Clerk Maxwell conducts an experiment to prove that light is a type of electromagnetic radiation. He predicts the existence of other kinds besides light.

1870 HYDROELECTRIC POWER
English engineer William Armstrong installs the first hydroelectric generator at Cragside in Northumberland, UK.

1882 POWER PLANT
The first public power plants open—one in London, UK and another in New York City. Both are powered by steam engines and each is the brainchild of American inventor Thomas Edison.

1884 STEAM TURBINE
Irish engineer Charles Algernon Parsons invents the steam turbine, an efficient steam engine that rotates very quickly. Today, steam turbines turn generators in most power plants.

1886 AUTOMOBILE
German engineer Karl Benz is granted a patent for the motor car. Within a few years, driving is popular, but only among the rich.

1887 RADIO WAVES
German physicist Heinrich Hertz discovers radio waves, whose existence was predicted by James Clerk Maxwell.

1887 WIND TURBINE
Scottish engineer James Blyth and American engineer Charles Brush independently become the first people to generate electricity using wind power.

1895 X-RAYS
German physicist Wilhelm Röntgen becomes the first to study a new mysterious form of electromagnetic radiation, which he calls X-rays.

1896 MORE MYSTERIOUS RAYS
French physicist Henri Becquerel discovers more strange invisible rays, which are produced by uranium.

1898 RADIOACTIVITY
French husband and wife Pierre and Marie Curie study Becquerel's rays, find them emanating from other elements, and coin the term "radioactivity."

1905 MASS ENERGY
As a consequence of his theory of Special Relativity, German physicist Albert Einstein discovers that energy and mass are directly linked. Mass can change into energy, and energy can turn into mass.

1930s ELECTRIFICATION
Most houses in developed countries are connected to the electric power grid by the end of the 1930s, after a huge program of electrification.

1942 FIRST NUCLEAR REACTOR
Italian-American scientist Enrico Fermi builds the world's first nuclear reactor in a sports hall at the University of Chicago.

1945 FIRST NUCLEAR WEAPON
American bomber airplanes drop the first atomic bomb on the Japanese city of Hiroshima, on August 6, immediately killing 80,000 people.

1954 SOLAR CELL
Technicians at Bell Laboratories develop the first modern "photovoltaic" solar cell.

Nuclear power plant at Calder Hall

1956 FIRST NUCLEAR POWER PLANT
The first commercial nuclear power plant opens at Calder Hall, England.

1965 BIG BANG
Scientists discover cosmic background radiation—heat radiation left over from about 300,000 years after the beginning of the universe, providing evidence for the Big Bang theory.

1990s GLOBAL WARMING
Scientists alert the public to the dangers of an excessive use of fossil fuels, which causes a rise in carbon dioxide levels in the atmosphere. Increased carbon dioxide seems to be causing a rise in the Earth's temperature.

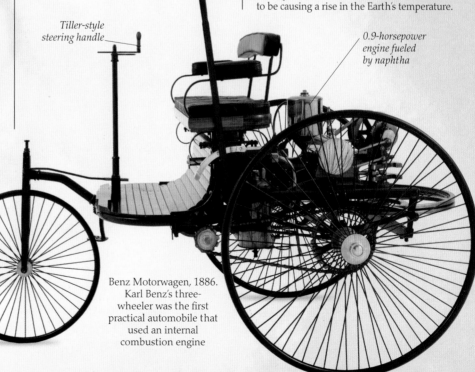

Tiller-style
steering handle

0.9-horsepower
engine fueled
by naphtha

Benz Motorwagen, 1886. Karl Benz's three-wheeler was the first practical automobile that used an internal combustion engine

Glossary

ALTERNATIVE ENERGY Sources of energy, normally used to generate electricity, that are alternatives to fossil fuels. Examples are solar power, wind power, and geothermal energy.

ATOM The smallest part of a chemical element; atoms are composed of smaller particles—protons, neutrons, and electrons. The number of protons defines what element the atom is—hydrogen has one proton, helium, two, for example.

AUTOTROPH A living organism that produces its own nutrients, normally using solar energy. The most important autotrophs are plants, which produce their own food by photosynthesis.

BIG BANG The theory that space and time—and energy—began billions of years ago as a tiny point, smaller than an atom, that expanded rapidly and has continued to do so ever since.

BIOMASS Biological material whose stored chemical potential energy can be used, typically to produce biogas or generate electricity.

CALORIE A unit of energy equivalent to the amount of heat required to increase the temperature of 1 gram of water by 1°C. The calorie is commonly used to list the energy of food. 1 kilocalorie = 4,184 joules.

CALORIMETER A scientific apparatus used for measuring the calorific value of fuels or foods.

COMBINED HEAT AND POWER An efficient approach to generating electricity with fossil fuels or nuclear power, in which heat that would otherwise be wasted is used to heat buildings.

COMBUSTION The scientific term for burning, in which chemical compounds combine with oxygen.

CONSERVATION OF ENERGY The theory that energy is never created nor destroyed. There is a fixed amount of energy available in the universe, and it merely changes its form.

COSMIC BACKGROUND RADIATION (CBR) Heat radiation produced when the universe was about 300,000 years old, and "stretched" by the expansion of space, so that what once was infrared radiation is now in the form of longer-wavelength microwaves.

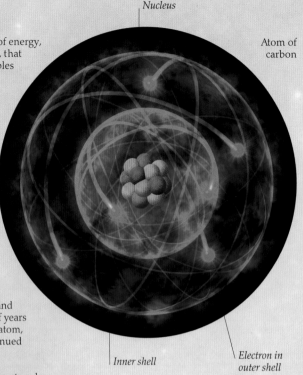

Nucleus

Atom of carbon

Inner shell

Electron in outer shell

DECOMPOSER A living thing that obtains the energy it needs to survive by breaking down dead organisms.

EFFICIENCY A measure of how much of the energy put into a process or device does the intended work. It is expressed as a percentage. When a muscle produces the force to move, 80 percent of the input energy is wasted as heat, so the efficiency of muscles is around 20 percent.

ELECTRIC CURRENT The movement of electrically charged objects. In a typical electric circuit, the moving objects are electrons, which move freely in certain materials, such as metals.

ELECTROMAGNETIC RADIATION The transfer of energy through space in the form of rippling electric and magnetic fields. Light, infrared, ultraviolet, radio waves, microwaves, X-rays, and gamma rays are all examples of electromagnetic radiation.

ELECTROMAGNETISM The combined effects of electricity and magnetism, in particular magnetism caused by electric currents and the currents produced by changing magnetic fields.

ELECTRON A tiny particle that carries a negative electric charge. Several or many electrons are found in every atom, and most electric currents are moving electrons.

ENERGY The ability to make things happen, or to "do work." The two main types of energy are potential energy and kinetic energy. (*See also* CONSERVATION OF ENERGY).

ENTROPY A measure of the state of randomness or disorder. A gas has much more entropy than a solid, because the particles of a gas fly around randomly at high speeds, while those in a solid vibrate around fixed positions.

FLUORESCENCE The production of visible light by certain substances when they are illuminated by ultraviolet radiation. Electrons in the atoms absorb energy from ultraviolet radiation, and emit the energy again as visible light.

FOSSIL FUEL A fuel that is a concentrated source of the chemical energy stored in living things that died millions of years ago. The main fossil fuels are coal, gas, and crude oil.

FREQUENCY The rate at which a recurring event happens. It is measured in "times per second," or hertz. It describes wave motion—with sound, a high-frequency wave vibrates the air thousands of times every second.

FRICTION A force produced between two objects rubbing together. Friction always produces heat—as in rubbing hands together.

GENERATOR A device for producing electrical energy from kinetic (movement) energy. Most generators contain rotating magnets or electromagnets inside coils of wire.

GEOTHERMAL ENERGY Useful heat energy extracted from deep underground that is used to heat buildings or to produce steam that turns turbines to generate electricity.

GLOBAL WARMING The slow but steady increase in the planet's average temperature, which climate scientists believe is caused largely by the increased levels of carbon dioxide that result from burning fossil fuels.

GREENHOUSE GAS Any atmospheric gas that absorbs infrared radiation that would otherwise escape to space. Carbon dioxide, water vapor, and methane are important greenhouse gases.

HEAT The transfer of internal energy from one substance to another—for example, from the Sun to Earth, by heat radiation. The word also means "thermal energy," which is the kinetic energy of the particles of matter.

Radio waves | Microwaves | Heat (infrared) | Ultraviolet | X-rays | Gamma rays

Visible light

Electromagnetic spectrum—the sequence of all possible forms of electromagnetic radiation

HYDROELECTRIC POWER The conversion of the kinetic energy of water to electrical energy, by turbines and generators.

HYDROGEN ECONOMY A possible way of making energy available on a huge scale in the future, using hydrogen as a fuel instead of fossil fuels. The product of burning hydrogen is water, with no carbon dioxide.

INCANDESCENCE The production of light by substances when they are hot. The orange and yellow parts of a candle flame glow through incandescence, as hot particles of carbon glow in the heat of combustion.

INFRARED RADIATION Electromagnetic radiation with a wavelength longer than red light. Human eyes are not sensitive to infrared radiation. Warm objects produce infrared radiation, which is also called heat radiation.

INTERNAL COMBUSTION ENGINE An engine in which fuel is rapidly burned inside cylinders, the explosions making pistons drive wheels or machinery.

JOULE The unit for measuring energy. Lifting a 100 gram apple 1 meter against Earth's gravity requires 1 joule of energy.

KINETIC ENERGY The energy of an object in terms of its motion. It depends on the mass of the object and its speed.

LATENT HEAT The heat energy required to melt a solid or vaporize a liquid. It is also the energy released when a gas condenses or a liquid solidifies.

MASS ENERGY According to Albert Einstein's Special Theory of Relativity, mass is a form of energy, and measured mass increases with an object's energy. At rest, an object has a "rest mass" given by the "m" in Einstein's famous equation, $E = mc^2$.

MOLECULE A tiny particle made of two or more atoms bonded together. Water is made of molecules consisting of two hydrogen atoms bonded to one oxygen atom (H_2O).

NUCLEAR FISSION A nuclear reaction in which a large atomic nucleus splits into two or more fragments, releasing energy. A nuclear power plant uses controlled nuclear fission to make steam, to turn generators.

NUCLEAR FUSION A nuclear reaction in which small atomic nuclei join together, or fuse, to form a larger one, often releasing energy. The Sun is powered by nuclear fusion reactions.

PARTICLE ACCELERATOR An apparatus in which powerful electric and magnetic fields accelerate electrically charged particles to

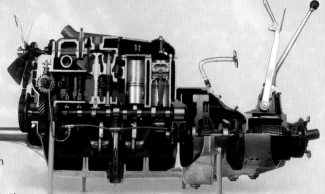

Internal combustion engine

high speeds. The particles collide into targets. Particles produced in the collisions can help scientists know more about matter.

PHOTOELECTRIC EFFECT A phenomenon in which electromagnetic radiation supplies energy to kick electrons out of their atoms, as a result of which they are free to flow as electric current.

PHOTOSYNTHESIS A very important set of chemical reactions that take place in certain organisms, particularly plants. The reactions are driven by energy from light (normally sunlight), which is converted to the chemical energy of sugar. (*See also* AUTOTROPH).

POTENTIAL ENERGY Stored energy, which is available to use in some form at a later time. A battery is a store of electrical potential energy.

POWER The rate at which energy is transformed from one form to another. It is usually measured in watts; 1 watt = 1 joule per second.

QUANTUM The smallest possible amount of energy in an event. Until the advent of this theory, scientists assumed that any amount of energy was possible, however small. But just as matter is made of particles, so is energy "quantized" in tiny amounts.

Model of a glucose molecule

RADIATION Energy transferred, or radiated in all directions. Normally, the term relates to electromagnetic radiation, such as light or microwaves.

RADIO WAVES A form of electromagnetic radiation with wavelengths longer than infrared radiation.

RADIOACTIVITY The release of energy by the breakup of unstable atomic nuclei. Such nuclei can emit alpha particles, beta particles, and gamma rays.

RENEWABLE ENERGY SOURCE Any source of energy that has no limit on its supply, unlike fossil fuels. Solar, geothermal, and wind energy are examples of this.

RESPIRATION Any set of chemical reactions, taking place inside a living organism, by which chemical energy stored in nutrients is made available to that organism.

SUSTAINABLE Able to continue forever without running out of energy or materials. Sustainable living includes recycling and making use of renewable energy sources.

TEMPERATURE A measure of how hot or cold a substance is. Scientifically, it is a measure of the average kinetic energy of the particles of a substance. As atoms and molecules are given more heat energy, they move more rapidly, and the temperature increases.

THERMODYNAMICS The scientific study of heat, temperature, and energy.

TURBINE A device that converts translational (straight ahead) motion into rotational motion. A wind turbine, for example, turns when the wind blows. Turbines connected to generators can generate electricity.

ULTRAVIOLET RADIATION Electromagnetic radiation with a wavelength slightly shorter than violet light. The Sun produces a great deal of ultraviolet radiation. (*See also* FLUORESCENCE).

VOLTAGE A measure of electrical potential energy. The potential of a battery to produce current is measured in volts, while the strength of an electric field is measured in volts per meter.

WATT A measure of power equal to one joule per second.

WAVE A regular motion in which energy is transferred through or across a substance. When a stone is dropped into a pond, for example, the kinetic energy disturbs the water, and the disturbance travels out in all directions, spreading out the energy across the pond.

WAVELENGTH The distance between two peaks (or troughs) in a wave. Although electromagnetic radiation travels as particles and waves, the different forms are distinguished by their different wavelengths. (*See also* RADIO WAVES, INFRARED, *and* ULTRAVIOLET RADIATION).

WORK Any process that requires energy. Scientists define work as a force multiplied by the distance through which it acts.

Model of the Hubble space telescope with solar panels

Solar panel

Index

Acknowledgments

Dorling Kindersley would like to thank:
John Becklake, Roger Bridgman, Neil Brown, Robert Bud, Clive Bunyan, Ian Carter, Robert Excell, Peter Fitzgerald, Graeme Fyffe, Mike Harding, Emma Hedderwick, Kevin Johnson, John Liffen, Peter Mann, Robert McWilliam, Steve Preston, Fiona Reid, Stephen Roberts, Derek Robinson, John Robinson, Ken Shirt, Victoria Smith, Peter Stephens, Ken Waterman, Jane Wess, Anthony Wilson, David Woodcock, and Michael Wright for advise and help with the provision of objects for photography at the Science Museum; Peter Griffiths for model making; Deborah Rhodes for page makeup; Karl Adamson, Paul Bricknell, Jane Burton, and Kim Taylor, Dave King, Tim Ridley, and Jerry Young for additional photography; The British Museum for photographing the central image on pp. 8–9; Solar Economy, Winchester, UK for providing the cutaway solar panel on p. 61; Peter Wilson, the Ministry of Agriculture, Norwich, for the loan of the calorimeter on p. 53.

Illustrations John Woodcock; **Cartography** Roger Bullen, James Mills-Hicks; **Proofreading** Sarah Owens; **Index** Jane Parker, Helen Peters.

The publisher would like to thank the following for their kind permission to reproduce their photographs:

(Key: a-above; b-below/bottom; c-center; f-far; l-left; r-right; t-top)

Alamy Images: Brand X Pictures 64–65, 66–67 (Background), 68–69, 70–71; Ingram Publishing 66bl; **Corbis**: Bettmann 69tl, 69tr, Julian Calverley 56b; Bettmann Archive 62bl. Bildarchiv Preussischer Kulturbesitz 30cl. British Film Institute 41cr; 45cl. Bulloz 52cr. Bruce Coleman 48tl; 56tl. Deutches Museum, Munich 42cl. **Dorling Kindersley**: Pearson Education 67tc, ESA 71br, National Motor Museum, Beaulieu 66crb, 69br, The Science Museum, London 68bl, 71tc, Tennis racquets courtesy of Wilson 67tl; **Dreamstime.com**: James Steidl 66bc, Zmaj011 66cl; Mary Evans Picture Library 7tr; 11tr; 14cl; 18cl; 20tl; 21cr; 30bl; 35tr; 38tl; 41tl; 43tl; 58cl.

Werner Foreman Archive 10tl. **Getty Images**: Steve Allen / Photodisc 64cl, Bloomberg 59tl, Hans Neleman / Stone 67tr, Leemage / Universal Images Group 68c; Giraudon 16br. Robert Harding Picture Library 35br; 61c. Michael Holford 30tl. Hulton Deutsche Picture Collection 16tl; 17tl; 24tr; 40cr; 45tr; 48br; 54tr. Hutchinson Library 10cl. Image Bank 53c. © King Features Syndicate Inc. 52tl. Mansell Collection 9cl. National Portrait Gallery 22tl. **NASA**: 31cr; 39cr; Scientific Visualization Studio Collection 67b; Novosti 44c. Pelizeus Museum, Hindelsheim 8bl. Philadelphia Museum of Art, Mr and Mrs Wharton Sinkler Collection 19cl. Planet Earth / Richard Coomer 6bl. Popperphoto 26bc. Ann Ronan at Image Select 11tr; 26cl. Royal Society 24cr. Professor S. Salter 59tr. Science Museum Photo Library 12tl; 13cr; 15bl; 29cr; 32cr; 38bl; 39tl; 42tl. Science Photo Library Keith Kent 6tl; /Stephen Dalton 17tr; /Simon Fraser 33cr; /Oscar Burriel 35bl; /Lecaque/ Roussel UCLAF/CNRI 36tl; 40tl; 45tr; / Los Alamos National Laboratory 46tl; /US Navy 47tr; /Hale Observatory 49tl; /Dr Ann Smith 52cl; /Lawrence Livermore Laboratory 56cl; /Anthony Howarth

57cr; /US Department of Energy 59cl; /Simon Fraser 59bl; /NASA 62bc. York Films of England 56br. Zefa 47bl; 59cr; 61tl.

With the exception of the items listed above, and objects on pages 6–7; 8–9; 10–11c; 14b; 15; 16–17tcl, c, and br; 19c; 21b and br; 23 tr; 24–25c; 27c; 37; 38–39c; 48–49 bl and c; 51 c and br; 52–53; 54c; 56–57; 60–61; 62–63, all the photographs in this book are of objects in the collections of the Science Museum, London.

Wall chart: Corbis: Image Source tr; **Dorling Kindersley**: ESA cl, The Science Museum, London tl, clb, bl, fbl, bc, cb, cra, fcra

Jacket: *Front*: **Dorling Kindersley**: Peter Griffiths—modelmaker tc, The Science Museum, London tl, ca; *Back*: **Dorling Kindersley**: Natural History Museum, London cl, The Science Museum, London ca, cra, c, bl

All other images © Dorling Kindersley
For further information, see: www.dkimages.com